Understanding your child through

ASTROLOGY

Understanding your child through
ASTROLOGY

by

DR. JOHN J. LOEPER

President, New Hope–Solebury (Pa.) Board of
School Directors
Principal, Blair Mill Elementary School, Hatboro (Pa.)

David McKay Company, Inc.   New York

to
Loretta Weller

Table of Contents

To the Reader

This book is not a substitute for love.

Neither is it a substitute for parental supervision, school guidance programs, professional psychological assistance.

It is not a book for predicting the future or for the abandonment of reason and free will.

I leave to professional astrologers the complex system of casting horoscopes and charting heavenly revolutions.

And I look with some disdain at the carefully nurtured mystique of astrological wizardry.

But I refuse to discard the obvious truthfulness of the universal character traits identified with specific sun signs. Time and time again, in my dealings with youngsters, I have been amazed at the accuracy of the personality profiles described by those astrological signs.

All I am saying in this book is that you, as a parent or teacher, must seriously consider the strong possibility that astrological speculation may be of some help to you in understanding your children. Then, it is your obligation to use this understanding to make of them healthier, happier, and more successful human beings.

1

Astrology and Me

Tears trickled down Janie's cheeks onto the spelling book on her desk directly in front of me.

Since the class was almost over, I quickly decided not to embarrass the eight-year-old by asking for an explanation. She continued to weep quietly and I continued to teach disconcertedly.

As soon as the class was dismissed, I walked over to the girl, put my arm around her and asked:

"Janie, dear, why are you crying?"

"My grandma! She died!" the child sobbed.

"My heavens," I said. "I didn't realize that. Why didn't your parents tell me? When did it happen?"

"Last year, I think," Janie answered.

I almost lost my temper. "Well, why are you crying now, in the middle of my spelling class?" I asked.

"Because I was just sitting here, thinking of her," Janie said.

I suppressed my annoyance because obviously the child was so sincere. Then, I considered her behavior.

"Pisces!" I thought. Typical Pisces behavior. One of the easiest sun signs to recognize and one of the hardest to deal with.

Perhaps you are shocked that I, an educator with advanced degrees, a school administrator, a member of a board of school directors, should in any way seriously consider the astrological signs of students. Well, I don't blame you. Until a few years ago, I, too, was one of the millions of people who considered astrology a potentially dangerous parlor game.

I had little respect for anyone who took it seriously. It was at best an amusement, I felt, and had little meaning in the serious duties of daily living. I ridiculed its scientific pretense and marveled at the gullibility of some of my believing friends.

Then, one day in 1958, I was introduced to a fascinating and highly intelligent individual. Among her other accomplishments, she was an amateur astrologer and she offered to describe my personality. I was dumbfounded by her accuracy. We had just met yet it seemed that she had known me for years and years. Here were some of my most private feelings and hidden fears being discussed at a first meeting. She gave a thorough description of me.

At first, I suspected that it was a combination of chance and keen observation. But the more I listened to her, the more fascinated I became. She discussed astrology intelligently and broke down the barriers of my own prejudice. She convinced me that astrology might have some validity and purpose.

After that, I borrowed several books from her library on astrology and began to study the subject. Before long, I was applying what I read to my family and my associates. Astrology seemed to work at every turn and I no longer took it lightly. I developed a respect for its ability to analyze those about me and help me to understand their behavior.

Gradually, but surely, I was becoming convinced that astrology could be a valuable tool in understanding people.

As a student of history, I had known of astrology's ancient significance in the story of man but it seemed to belong to the age of superstition and magic. I did not think it belonged in a scientific age.

As a student of psychology, I realized that each of us is motivated in our own unique way yet controlled by certain common desires and drives. But I would not admit to the universal influence of the heavens. It was not until I began using astrology pragmatically that I began to be converted from my skepticism.

Then, in one of my English classes, I began to become aware of the personality problem of 14-year-old Eric. He was moody—subject to periods of euphoria and periods of depression. One day he might be friendly and outgoing; the next day he would be unfriendly and uncooperative.

"Just like me!" I thought to myself. I'm constantly fighting off a tendency to give in to my many moods. "I bet he's a Cancer, too."

Just for the fun of it, I checked his birthdate on the records. It was true!

Then, in continuation of the game, I tried to pick out the other Cancers in the class. I was right 80% of the time! Soon, it reached a point where I was almost inevitably correct in identifying others of my sign.

I found, too, that I was able to communicate with Eric a bit better because I knew more of his character traits that were not instantly apparent. I found myself a little more compassionate and understanding.

So, after using astrology successfully in my private life, I had found that I could carry it over into my professional life. I took astrology to school. More and more, I began to use the sun sign characteristics in approaching my students and in helping them with their problems. I had a tool more useful than any other I had previously used. I began to understand more clearly the motivations and weaknesses of my students and I developed a sincere appreciation for the sun sign personalities.

I found that you handle a Cancer child one way and a Scorpio in another way. I discovered that the guidance of astrology in assignments, expectations, and actual achievement was incredibly effective. I was no longer annoyed and frustrated over the characteristics of certain pupils because I understood more of the "why" of their behavior and reactions.

Obviously, I never revealed what I was doing. After all, educated people are not supposed to subscribe to such esoteric beliefs and most men of learning have scant regard for astrology. Considering my former attitudes, I realized this all too well. For, despite its long and honorable history, the academic world has chosen to ignore a study that has helped to explain human behavior for centuries. Most will not even pay it the courtesy of a casual investigation.

Yet, what I was doing worked. I was meeting with success in education and receiving recognition for it—but I still felt I couldn't reveal one of my methods. Although my fellow professionals recognized this success, they would have ridiculed me if I had shared this method with them.

Finally, now, after more than ten years of observing sun signs as they are reflected in the personalities of young people, I am convinced that the time is ripe to present my ideas. I want others to know that there is a great body of information in astrological sun signs waiting to be recognized—and utilized.

I use astrology for my private information. I have never attempted to substitute it for any other authentic, established avenue of helping children. I use it strictly as a supplement to my store of background information.

I am convinced that you also have the right—perhaps even the obligation—to investigate astrology as yet another method of helping you to understand your own children.

2

A Short History of Astrology

Mark hates school and is embarrassed whenever the teacher calls on him. His birthday is May third and that makes him a Taurus. He's behaving normally for his particular sun sign.

Julie will begin kindergarten next September. She was born on July tenth. Her mother can expect tears and protests when she leaves her at the classroom door. Julie is a Cancer child and will not relish being pushed out of the nest.

Edgar never gets to school on time. He finds all sorts of diversions along the way to detain him. Not too unusual for a Gemini youngster.

Astrology helps in understanding children and why not? It has a long and distinguished history in its service to man. It is really the summation of over 5000 years of observation and experience. It was studied by the ancient Egyptians, Assyrians, and Chinese. Both kings and common folk would rarely make an important decision without consulting the astrologers. The Egyptians accumulated great reference libraries filled with astrological lore and the Chinese built an intricate astrological clock to tell heavenly time. And those three wise men from the East who followed a strange star to Bethlehem were really astrologers.

Astrology pervaded the ancient world and was an accepted science. It studied human behavior and claimed that personality patterns were determined by the position of the stars and planets at the time of birth. It insisted that cosmic forces influence the behavior of man.

Astrology spread to Rome and Greece and was used by physicians and philosophers. Several Roman books in the field of astrology have survived. Notable among these is the *Four Books on the Influence of the Stars* by Claudius Ptolemy.

In the New World, the Mayans and the Aztecs built observatories to study the heavens. They used astrology to predict the weather and did it so accurately that astrology became a part of their religious beliefs. To the ancient people, astrology was the communication of the gods and the language of heaven.

During the Middle Ages, astrology lived comfortably with Christianity. Popes and kings used the guidance of the stars to aid in the government of their realms and the court astrologer was an important political figure. One of the most famous of these was Michel de Notre Dame, better known as Nostradamus. He served as an astrologer to three French kings and wrote a long series of poems predicting future events in world history. He is said to have predicted the invention of the airplane, the submarine, and the discovery of atomic power.

Many of the famous names of medieval Europe are associated with astrology. Thomas Aquinas, Albertus Magnus, Dante, and Chaucer were among the scholars who investigated the heavenly forces. Men like Copernicus and Johannes Kepler believed in the influence of the stars on human affairs. Kepler wrote, "We cannot deny the influence of the stars without disbelieving in the wisdom of God." Galileo, the father of modern astronomy, was a scientist-astrologer, as was John Dee, the English mathematician.

Astrology was widely accepted in Elizabethan England. Elizabeth I took lessons in casting horoscopes and William Shakespeare makes numerous references to the influence of the stars. He speaks of Romeo and Juliet as "star-crossed lovers" and in *King Lear* he says, "The stars above us govern our conditions." Although Shakespeare never used the term "astrology," he makes over one hundred references to the potency of the stars.

That astrology has played a vital role in the history of the world would be difficult to deny. Royal families used it to determine the most auspicious date for weddings and coronations. It was even used to tell the most appropriate moment for conception and many monarchs would not approach Her Majesty's bedchamber without the approval of the astrologers!

Our own nation was "born" in July because Thomas Jefferson, himself a student of astrology, wanted the United States under the sign of Cancer.

Historical figures like Napoleon and Adolph Hitler employed astrology in their careers. During World War II, Louis De Wohl, an astrologer, was assigned by British Intelligence to inform the British of the advice Hitler was getting from his astrologer. In this way, the Allies had advance information on what he was likely to do. Using astrology, they outguessed some of his maneuvers and strategic military decisions. After the war, De Wohl was officially honored and recognized for his service.

Even the hard-headed financier, J. P. Morgan, used astrology in building his multi-million dollar empire. To this day, many Wall Street businessmen consult the stars for guidance in financial matters.

Astrology has been with mankind since the dawn of history. It has disappeared several times but has always enjoyed a revival. Surviving abuse and assault, it has always reappeared like the Phoenix rising from the ashes. It is enjoying a fresh popularity during our present space age. From Detroit to Berlin, magazines and newspapers carry astrological columns and most large cities have their share of professional astrologers. One famous astrologer boasts of casting over 3000 horoscopes a year and others now utilize the computer. Astrology, in offering a theory of astral influence, has a certain appeal for modern man—it assures him of an individuality and an identity in this numbered age.

The moon landing, too, has brought man into closer touch with the cosmos. Deep down in the inner sanctums of the human spirit, there is a conviction that we are somehow a part of the universe and share in its allness. Astrology offers us this assurance.

Astrology is usually divided into three main branches. One is called Judicial Astrology, and this gives an individual's characteristics based on the time of birth. A second is called Horary Astrology, and gives day-to-day advice. An example of this is the daily astrology columns featured in newspapers. A third branch is Natural Astrology, and deals with national and worldwide events. Our prime concern in this book will be with Judicial Astrology.

The basis of Judicial Astrology is the sun sign. This is the sign of birth. It places a person under one of the twelve signs of the Zodiac. It is the first key to character and gives the basic characteristics of personality. The sun sign denotes the position of the sun at the time of birth according to the astrological movement of the heavens. The sun exerts the strongest influence of any of the heavenly bodies and is the starting point for character analysis. Although the other stars and planets have influence, the sun sign is the strongest force. The twelve signs of the Zodiac, or the twelve positions of the sun during the calendar year, are:

Aries the Ram—March 21 to April 20
Taurus the Bull—April 21 to May 21
Gemini the Twins—May 22 to June 21
Cancer the Crab—June 22 to July 23
Leo the Lion—July 24 to August 23
Virgo the Virgin—August 24 to September 23
Libra the Scales—September 24 to October 23
Scorpio the Scorpion—October 24 to November 22
Sagittarius the Archer—November 23 to December 21
Capricorn the Goat—December 22 to January 20
Aquarius the Water-Bearer—January 21 to February 19
Pisces the Fish—February 20 to March 20

These are the approximate dates when the sun moves from one sign to another. The first and last dates may be slightly in error from year to year only because our calendar is imperfect. Consequently, if you were born on August 21, you might be either a Leo or a Virgo. Most likely you will have qualities of both signs. Remember too that the influence of the receding sign lingers on into the beginning period of the next, and the end period of that sign is influenced by the rising one. If a birthdate is at the beginning or end of a sign period, this must be taken into consideration.

Keep in mind that the use of astrology without observation is useless. A person born on September 20 is a Virgo but will be influenced by the next sign of Libra. Likewise, someone born on July 24 falls under Leo, but will be influenced by the passing sign of Cancer. Being born at the beginning or end of a sign is referred to as being born on the cusp.

The sun sign places a person under certain influences which help shape the personality. As geographical location and climate play a role in human conditions, so does the position of the sun. According to astrology, the sun places us within a sphere that predisposes us to certain attributes and shortcomings. The sun sign inclines us to a temperament.

Through a knowledge of the sun signs, we can gain a better basic understanding of the people we are concerned about and a background that helps us to delve more deeply and understandingly into their personalities.

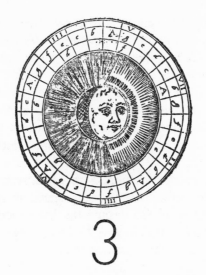

3

Education and Astrology

Edward suddenly developed an aversion to school.

This 12-year-old had always been a good student and had a fine record of cooperating with his teachers. Now he was a problem child!

His teacher complained that Edward refused to do his assignment work and sulked most of the day. He was sullen and depressed. His teacher was exasperated and she claimed that nothing she did seemed to work. It certainly wasn't her fault—she was absolutely certain of that!

I checked both their sun signs and immediately suggested that Edward be transferred to another class. As soon as he was assigned to a new teacher, Edward's attitude changed almost completely.

Certainly, it was obvious that there had been a personality conflict—the teacher later admitted that she "had to force myself to like him." But, it was a personality conflict that could have been predicted. Edward was a Cancerian and the teacher was a Sagittarian. These two signs simply do not mix, in or out of the classroom.

It has been my experience that many classroom problems are due to sign conflicts. Of course, referring to it as a "personality conflict" is more acceptable to educators. But a sign conflict is exactly what it is—and a sign conflict can be predicted.

This is part of the usefulness of astrology in education. It allows you to assess the mixing of personalities before the actual mixing takes place. It puts the horse before the cart and avoids potential problems by allowing you to create an environment in which signs can flourish. In assigning students to teachers, how many conflicts could be averted through the application of astrology!

As an educator I have been exposed to hundreds of theories about child development and behavior. Like so many teachers and parents, I frequently find myself in a sea of confusion amid all the theories and practices. In the school business, the pendulum swings back and forth and what was in vogue yesterday is old hat today, only to enjoy a new popularity tomorrow. Every day a "new" theory or a "unique" idea is presented by experts. The conflict of opinion is rampant as one advises us to do this while another advises us to do that.

Out of all this, the best one can do is to try to sift out the grains of truth from all sources and apply them to personal experience. And yet amid all this conflict and confusion, there remains an art-science that has weathered the storms of centuries. It doesn't change and it doesn't contradict itself. It states its premises and declares them workable despite the time and place. Astrology.

Astrology is really the experience of the ages and if it can assist us in understanding the complexities of human behavior, then why not use it? I have discovered through experience that the sun sign characteristics have been of immense help in understanding children. Astrology has explained more to me than modern orthodox theories of personality and explained it more humanly because it teaches that we are not all alike. The notion of "individual difference," so dear to the hearts of educators, is ancient history to astrology.

I have heard psychologists and educators ascribe certain personality characteristics to different body types. The ectomorph, the endomorph, and the mesomorph all behave in different ways. The ectomorph has a narrow, fragile body and is said to be a sensitive, artistic person. The endomorph is the chubby, soft individual said to be less active and inclined to self-indulgence. The mesomorph is the active, energetic, square, hard body.

I have heard children described as under-achievers, overachievers, introverts, and extroverts. I have seen educators play with test score numbers to describe children.

There always seems to be an available label to describe behavior and every new system that comes down the pike is embraced with eager affection. We love to pigeonhole people, yet the astrological categories are labeled as nonsense by most professionals. Could it be that astrology has been teaching what science is just discovering—that certain people share common traits due to common factors?

We know that the seasons and the weather have a direct effect on mind and body. I am not the same person on a cold, dismal, gray winter day that I am on a bright, sunny morning in June. The School of Pathology of the University of Illinois carried on extensive studies on the influence of weather upon health and published its findings in many volumes. According to many scientists, human progress is accelerated in a moderate climate and slowed down in extreme climates. Could it be that the season of our birth does have an influence on personality? Several years ago an educational research team conducted a study that indicated that children born during the winter months achieved significantly better grades in school than those born during the summer months.

Science is learning more and more about new forces of energy. The laser beam, atomic radiation, and space science have added much to our understanding of the universe. Years ago we believed that atomic structure could not be altered; today we know otherwise. We are learning more about genetics, and some scientists see the day when we will be able to change genetic structure and produce an individual of our own design. We are finding that folk medicine and herbal lore contain truths now accepted by modern medicine. Perhaps the same is true of astrology.

Is it possible that the energies of outer space influence personality and behavior? Could it be that we are guided by the stars under which we were born as astrology says? Someday, astrology may be seriously investigated by modern science and tested under control. Then, perhaps, it will be dignified with a respected place among the branches of knowledge.

There is no one science that explains man. All sciences and all philosophies come into play in a discussion of human behavior. Astrology offers another dimension in understanding. It is another door to be opened and another path to be followed in dealing with humans.

I do not suggest it as a daily guide or as a means of predicting the future. I do not totally accept it in this way. I do suggest, however, that it can be a valuable tool in working with people.

Neither do I want astrology to take the place of accepted practice in understanding and guiding children. This would be madness. I suggest that astrology should be used with other approaches to understand and comprehend better the complexities of the human personality. Every body of knowledge has a place and function in the study of man and anything that deepens understanding and adds dimension cannot be rejected. The study of man is a science; the study of living is an art. Astrology combines the two into a workable pattern.

Through my many years in education, I have become sure of one thing: motivation is the most important factor in teaching. If a person can be motivated, he can learn anything. Without motivation, regardless of ability, he cannot learn.

One of the greatest educational experiments ever undertaken had its genesis in the G.I. Bill of Rights, which followed World War II. Masses of veterans were sent back to schools and colleges at that time by the Government. Many of them had failed in school and, according to school records and test results, were labeled as failures. Yet, today, the professions and skilled trades are filled with these so-called "failures."

What happened? They were motivated to learn! They *wanted* to learn and they did. The magic ingredient of their success was their own desire to succeed.

The same holds true for youngsters in school. A pupil succeeds because he wants to. I have known youngsters who were labeled "unteachable," suddenly to become alive and achieve. What happened? The same answer—they were motivated, either by some inner drive or by the clever handling of a good teacher. The master teacher is really the master of motivation.

Mankind has always been concerned with motivation. What makes a person behave as he does? What moves him into action? Why do two people in similar circumstances react in different ways? Two women witness the same accident. One screams and goes to pieces. The other remains calm and offers help. There have been all sorts of answers.

The ancients ascribed it to the whims of the gods and later religions found answers within their beliefs.

With the advent of twentieth-century psychology, there were attempts to explain motivation scientifically. There was the drive theory of motivation that had man respond to his basic drives, expressed either in actuality or in disguise. The need for water motivated the thirsty man and some dreams were an expression of the sex drive. Then, the notion of secondary drives was introduced. These are drives that are learned through association with a basic need. The baby associates mother and food, or a man learns to associate fear with some object or event.

Freud claimed that motivation had its roots in the unconscious. He said that we are motivated by events, frustrations, and anxieties stored in our unconscious mind.

At present, other theories of motivation are being formulated. There are theories involving external stimulation, brain chemistry, and genetic patterns. All are trying to discover why people do what they do.

Educators also type children for easy reference. Ernest Kretschmer, the German psychologist, gave us personality types based on body build. His studies indicated that the short, stout people, or "pyknic" type was prone to manic-depression, whereas the tall, thin type, or "leptosome" was prone to schizophrenia. Later, W. H. Sheldon structured a seven-step scale based on body build to measure patterns of temperament.

In the twentieth century, Dr. Carl G. Jung coined the terms extrovert and introvert as the opposite poles of personality. Then, Louis Berman gave us personality types based on the secretions of the endocrine glands. One of his types, the "adrenal personality," was characterized as outgoing, energetic, and efficient. Recent attempts to type personalities have ranged from G. W. Allport's work to the development of projective tests. Allport described individual traits as being in a hierarchy, with some stronger than others. Projective tests mark their beginning with Herman Rorschach's ink blots. According to Rorschach, a person's description of ink blots gives clues to his creativity and emotional balance.

Today, there are hundreds of these projective tests being used to describe personality. They range from drawing pictures to association responses. Personality inventories are also used to group people. One, the Minnesota Multiphasic Inventory, uses approximately 500 questions to type the personality.

Despite the variety of techniques available, most educators admit that it is very difficult to measure personality. Yet most steadfastly refuse to apply astrology as a tool. They would rather put their faith in variable theory or surrealistic patterns. Many critics have called the personality testing done today "immoral and inaccurate."

Mike is under the sun sign of Pisces. This tells us that he has an active imagination. The projective test phrased it as "prone to fantasy." Julia is an Aquarian. As such, she has a low boiling point and loses her temper quickly. The projective test said that she has a "low frustration level." Projective test results frequently uphold astrological descriptions. "John's difficulties in learning are related to a loss of concentration rather than any deficit in native intelligence," reads the report. John is a Gemini and is inclined to weak powers of concentration. Personality tests seem to support the sun sign traits.

It is quite obvious that any improved understanding of personality will result in an improved understanding of motivation.

Billy is a Capricorn child and the appeal to him will be through his desire to please those in authority. Ronald is a Sagittarius and the same appeal might be ineffective. Astrology helps us to understand personality by giving us time-tested clues to child behavior.

If personality really holds the key to motivation, then an understanding of astrology should be of enormous interest to education.

4

Psychology and Astrology

"Astrology is the summation of all the psychological knowledge of antiquity."

What mystic crackpot made that outrageous statement, you ask? Only Dr. Carl G. Jung, a student of Freud, and the world famous psychiatrist who dared to suggest that astrology and psychology might be branches of the same science and serve one another.

"The fact that it is possible to construct a person's character from the data of his nativity shows the validity of astrology," he said. "I believe in it because it works."

In his book, *The Interpretation of Nature and the Psyche*, Jung published an astrological experiment which he had conducted. He took 400 married couples and had a horoscope cast for each husband and wife. He then examined these horoscopes and discovered many obvious similarities. To his amazement he found that, without using the guidance of astrology, many of these couples had instinctively selected the mate that astrology would have suggested. Here was a case where astrology and human instinct worked hand in hand.

Dr. Jung realized that astrology was a valuable tool and had a functional use in psychiatry. He hired an astrologer as a member of his staff and he studied his patient's horoscopes. He found that a knowledge of their sun signs helped in better understanding their behavior. A case history included astrological data. Jung felt that astrology helped him to understand complications in character and gave him an additional point of view. He tried to encourage his fellow professionals to use astrology in their practice but he was not successful.

Scientists seem to resist anything that is an old belief, thinking that what is old must also be false. It is most unfortunate that modern science refuses to re-examine ancient wisdom in the light of modern knowledge. Some have found the courage to do so, but their number is small.

In trying to understand human behavior, psychology has turned to rats and dogs, to mazes and tests. During its very short history, for it is a young science—it has tried to help us understand ourselves.

The first school of psychologists were the structuralists. They were formed about 1880 and held that the human mind could be analyzed through introspection. They believed that conscious experience was composed of inner sensations, images, and feelings.

A later group called themselves the functionalists. They believed that man should be studied in his attempt to adjust to his environment.

A third group were the behaviorists. They turned to man's overt behavior and concentrated on conditioned response experiments.

Then, under the leadership of Sigmund Freud, came the

school of psychoanalysis. The emphasis of psychoanalysis was on the unconscious mind.

In the 1920's, the Gestalt school was formed. They believed that the whole of experience and behavior must be studied in order to understand man. The word Gestalt means "pattern" in German.

In our present day, we have many new schools of thought in psychology. One, for example, concentrates on an individual's self-image and uses this as a framework for understanding behavior.

The psychologist and Nobel Prize winner, Charles Richet, did work in clairvoyance and precognition. Other serious scientists and researchers are examining herbal medicine, acupuncture, weather lore, and folk superstition. Out of some of this research may come new knowledge. Over the years, architects have learned construction techniques by examining ancient structures; doctors have discovered new cures by investigating old remedies; geographers have uncovered data by studying old maps; and artists have found the old pigments of the masters more durable than today's. What is old is not always useless, and what is new is not always best.

Although the various schools of psychology may disagree on certain points, they all share the fundamental aim of psychology—the understanding of man and his behavior. Astrology shares the same goal.

Psychologists, in studying human behavior, are finding out that individuals can be grouped according to certain personality traits. They are also finding out that certain people, given the same set of circumstances, will react in much the same way. Could it be that psychology is discovering what astrology has always taught?

Psychology is finding that some behavior is predictable. Astrology has been teaching this for centuries. It would be a great benefit to mankind if these two studies could join forces, as Jung suggested, and share in an understanding of man. Psychology and astrology study the same subject—the behavior of people—and many times they reach the same conclusions using different roads. Perhaps astrology is really psychology and psychology is really astrology!

The ancients may not have been aware of our modern methods and techniques but, using astrology, they successfully categorized and synthesized the human personality. Their efforts were subjected to the examination and application of centuries. Their explanations may be in error but their theories seem to work. No matter how often astrology has been attacked and vilified, it has survived the assault. Its endurance alone is evidence of its strength. If it did not work and had proved useless, it probably would have withered and died away long ago. It is the new discovery of its truth by each generation that seems to keep it alive.

There are some people who have made serious attempts to examine and use astrological information in the professions. But those who have are reluctant to publish their findings because they fear the scorn of their peers. Astrology has been forced to wear the dunce cap for so long that it has taken on an aura of foolishness and hocus-pocus. If you keep astrology in the parlor, you're safe. As long as it's an innocent little pastime, your friends and associates will indulge your idiosyncrasy. After all, even the best of men has a foible or two. It's when you begin to take it seriously or recognize a daily application that you're in deep water.

I do not deny that there is a lunatic fringe who use astrology for every purpose under the sun. Nor do I deny the misconceptions and fanciful claims made by many practitioners. I find much in astrology that I cannot accept. I do believe, however, in its hypothesis that different effects are produced by different seasons of birth. I find it easily plausible that cosmic forces may be transmitted to the earth and have a qualifying effect on human behavior. It is consistent with my personal philosophy, which recognizes a harmony and relationship between every entity in the universe.

Perhaps if astrology were given a new name, it might win additional support among professionals in psychology. Now, it struggles along fearing the vices and virtues of its past. And its vices are more noticeable. If astrology were ever proved legitimate through controlled research, there would be a lot of embarrassed "experts." Often, those who condemn and mock astrology have scant knowledge about it, and stubbornly refuse to examine what they so freely attack.

There is much in astrology that may be superstition, but there is much that may be wisdom. The German poet Goethe wrote, "Astrology has its beginning in a remote sense of some great cosmic unity. We know that the heavenly bodies have an influence on weather and the growth of plants. Carrying this further, who can say where this influence stops?"

Scholars have long recognized the unity of the universe and the interrelationship of things within that universe. There is an order and harmony that blends into a grand design. They search for that one ultimate law that will encompass the universe and reveal the last great secret. To deny truth in astrology or any other art or science is to close avenues of enlightenment and discovery. Ancient concepts must be examined again and again for truth and knowledge. No expression of human thought should ever be discarded with haughty disdain.

Psychologists, in particular, should be sympathetic to that point of view. And, in general, they are. Except it seems, where astrology is involved.

5

Your Child and Astrology

Since astrology has become a subject of major interest to youngsters, a teacher in one of my grades assigned the topic of sun signs as a class project. Each student was supposed to identify his own sun sign and tell whether or not it fit him.

One youngster, looking very disturbed, raised his hand after doing some research in a library book on astrology.

"Sir," he said, "the book says my sun sign is Scorpio and it's supposed to rule the private parts."

"That's correct," the teacher answered warily.

"Well, could you please tell me where mine are?" he asked.

I tell this story to indicate just how widespread is the popular fascination for astrology. It has spread even to those young enough (and, perhaps, naive enough) to be uncertain about the location of their "private parts."

The chances are that whether or not *you* decide to try to use astrological information in helping your child toward a healthy personality, *he* may decide to use it himself. So, why not make the effort first?

However, always keep in mind that a child's sun sign may help to delineate his personality, but it does not fulfill his personality. To make any potential an actuality requires effort and determination. Astrology tells us what *can* be, not what *must* be. The must is up to us. Astrology can become an insidious crutch if it is used to excuse behavior or when it takes on a dogmatic determinism. It serves a purpose only when it enhances our understanding.

The responsibility of parenthood makes only one demand —that we love our children. Any additional responsibilities are added by our own individual social or economic advantage. Nature does not demand the best schools, the finest clothing, and the most expensive toys. These, without love, are useless.

A child is terribly vulnerable. From the first year of life, he must trust those around him. He is at the mercy of their attitudes and their limitations. He must reach out to them for security and affection, and they will give him only what they can give. If they are incapable of love, the child will receive none. If they are bitter and dejected, the child will suffer. Delinquency records are full of cases like this. Despite comfortable homes and social privileges, many youngsters grow up anxious and insecure. Although their personalities may have been blessed by the sun, they have been warped by their experiences on earth.

During these critical, formative years, a child is totally dependent on others. For this reason, it is vital that parents find love in themselves and work hard to make marriage a success. You cannot give children what you do not have yourself. More than anything else, a child needs a happy home and loving parents. If there is tension and turmoil between parents, the child will sense it and respond accordingly. As he grows and matures, he will become increasingly aware of the emotional atmosphere of his home and of the relationships of those around him. His responses and attitudes will begin to crystallize as he observes and reacts to his environment. And even a domestic Cancerian can learn to hate an unhappy home and a warm Libran can chill in a climate of rejection and hostility.

Fostering a healthy personality and helping your child develop the assets of his sun sign requires good, loving parents. However, the degree of love must change as the child matures. A child's emotional needs change as he grows. He is not as dependent on his parents at twelve as he was at three. The wise parents will recognize the increasing desire for independence as the years roll by and make adjustments in their relationships with children. They will begin to slacken the apron strings and allow for individuality and exploration. Children may experience rough waters on this journey toward adulthood, but this is to be expected.

Sometimes, children may seem to rebel against the world and reject the standards we have given them. They become sloppy, non-conformist, and antagonistic. This is just their way of declaring independence. Underneath it all, they still crave parental support and guidance. To recognize this and understand it will help you to live with it. There can be many lopsided kinds of love and these are as dangerous as none at all. Growing up also means growing away.

Good parents want their children to grow up emotionally and physically healthy. They want them to develop their personal assets and learn to underplay the liabilities and be free of any traits that might spoil a meaningful adult life. They want them to live well, love well, work well, and find fulfillment. The sun signs of astrology can assist in this seemingly overwhelming job by pointing out the likely virtues and flaws of personality.

The sun signs, however, do not imply a disregard for common sense. Parents will find no quick solutions or easy answers in astrology. They will instead find guidance and direction, but they must supply the balance, humor, and love necessary in solving their problems and in meeting everyday situations. To say that a Taurus child is stubborn by nature is an understanding. To say that there is nothing to be done in controlling this stubbornness is a misunderstanding. The sun signs give direction, but we take the journey.

Nor does astrology negate the virtues of a good life. Truthfulness, consideration for others, self-reliance, unselfishness, generosity, and fairness are still desirable traits in everyone. To use the sun signs to sweep away any of these would be foolish. They merely indicate how easy or difficult the task of teaching these virtues will be.

Accepting children as children is the first step in understanding them. We must recognize them as growing, developing, searching humans endowed with potentialities and limitations. We must give them love and freedom, structure and flexibility. We want them to live wisely and vigorously and be self-controlled without being restricted. We want them to inherit the legacy of our culture, our nation, our families, and their own sun-designed personalities.

6

Your Child's Sun Sign Profile

From my reading, research, and experience, I will attempt to describe the characteristics of the various sun signs as they apply to children. Obviously, the child responds differently from the adult. The astrological qualities of youngsters are not those of the mature sign. The young Leo is not the mature Leo, nor is the young Taurus as clearly defined as the old Taurus. Children are immature in every way.

I also suggest methods of discipline to be used with each sign. As parents know only too well, not every method works equally well with every child. Hopefully, the sun sign advice will guide you in knowing which discipline technique is best for your child. I also try to offer additional astrological advice in academic preferences and future careers.

Remember that a youngster born at the beginning or end of a sign span—with his sun in a cusp or borderline position—will be influenced by the other sign. For these youngsters, you must study both signs and allow your observation to determine the dominant characteristics.

Never underestimate the value of your own observation as a parent. Astrology helps you only to interpret this observation and make it more meaningful.

It must also be pointed out that the qualities of each sign can be expressed in either a positive or a negative manner. Moral training, environment, and heredity help determine this. Characteristics can be used to advantage or disadvantage. There is an old saying that the stars "do not command, they direct." Astrology gives the tendencies, the directions, and the leanings. How each individual applies these in his daily living is a matter of free choice.

For example, Cancer makes an excellent parent but the individual determines whether she will give mother love or smother love! And the leadership qualities of a Leo can lead others toward good or evil.

If you place a child within the frame of his sun sign, other information begins to fall into place and becomes meaningful. It's important to remember that it is just a framework and not dogma. It is another path to deeper understanding.

Also, remember that individuality reigns supreme. You are always dealing with a unique human being with a unique background. Think of sun sign descriptions as stage settings. The individual child develops the script and the action. Remember that I am speaking of understanding the normal child. Those children with special problems must always be specially handled.

Astrology can help you become a better parent by helping you to understand your child. The personality traits of the

sun signs should be used as guidance in raising your youngster. But, remember that astrology is only a help—it is up to
you and the way you handle your knowledge to see to it that
your child develops into a healthy, positive-thinking and
morally fit individual.

How to Interpret Sun Sign Information

Sun sign characteristics tend to be most correct if your
child was born dead-center of his sign. The influence of the
preceding sign will affect his characteristics if he was born in
the early portion of the sign; the influence of the following
sign will affect his characteristics if he was born late in the
sign.

Most astrologers refer to the four days before and the four
days after as the cusp—or borderline—thus, the Pisces-Aries
cusp would be the period from March 17 through March
25. The Aries-Taurus cusp would be the period from April 17
through April 25.

Some astrologers consider that the influence of the preceding and following signs extend much deeper into the signs
and divide each sign into decanates—three equal parts. The
first third is influenced by the preceding sign, the second
third is more or less pure, the last third is influenced by the
following sign.

It has been my experience that the preceding and following
signs can play an even more important part in the sun sign
characteristics—right up to the dead center. Thus, I usually
pay close attention to the preceding sign for everybody born
in the first half of the sign, and the following sign for those
born in the final half. For instance, when I refer to Aries
(Pisces side) and Aries (Taurus side) I am referring to preceding and following signs. This information should be inte-
grated with the more universal characteristics listed under
the sun sign itself.

Astrologers usually agree on the four basic elements and what they symbolize for the persons born under their influence. Each sign is considered to be influenced in great part by one element.

Aries, Leo, Sagittarius: FIRE (ambition, enthusiasm, courage)

Libra, Aquarius, Gemini: AIR (sociability, intelligence)

Cancer, Scorpio, Pisces: WATER (sensitivity, mysticism, emotion)

Capricorn, Taurus, Virgo: EARTH (dependability, constructiveness, power)

your child the

aries

march 21–april 20
symbol:

the ram

ruling planet: **mars** • element: **fire**

POSITIVE CHARACTERISTICS:
Spontaneity, enterprise, decisiveness

NEGATIVE CHARACTERISTICS:
Impatience, boastfulness, domination

GETS ALONG BEST WITH:
Sagittarius, Leo

Jack, be nimble,
Jack, be quick,
Jack, jump over the candlestick.

Jack Aries loves a challenge and a chance to prove his superiority.

35

New ventures and undertakings are joys to the Arien child. He will probably look forward to the start of another school year. This is a new adventure and he often approaches it with great expectations, although not necessarily in the academic area. His interest is more in the anticipated fun and friendship of school life. The Arien child wants to get back to the old gang and his playground cronies. He is usually excited over the social aspect of school rather than any instructional one.

The playground is his kingdom and recess games are his special delight. He wants to be leader and likes to take charge. In a game, he is often the captain of the team. If not, then he enjoys giving orders to everyone, including whomever might be the team captain! The Arien boy is a natural for Little League and the Arien girl will most likely run her Brownie troop.

But if Aries likes to demonstrate his superiority, he loses interest quickly. When he is finished with something, he is finished! He loves to dash into new ventures but sometimes at the expense of past commitments. He might suddenly walk off the Little League team to join the Boy Scouts and no amount of coaxing or threats will change his mind. One Arien girl decided that her 4-H group was "stupid." Despite the fact that she was its most distinguished member, she walked out. And never expect Ariens to rationalize these sudden decisions.

The Arien child takes no interest in organization and detail. He likes to live in a casual manner and has a lusty appreciation for fun and frolic.

Aries is active, energetic, and freedom-loving. He loves life and sees no need for taking it too seriously. For this very reason, parents and teachers can expect no sterling academic record from an Arien child. If he is interested in a particular subject, you will have no worries. He will bring home good grades on his report card. But, should he decide he doesn't like the subject, or even worse, the teacher, then all effort will come to a sudden halt. He can learn easily and get good grades—if he wants to! More than likely, he will love history, especially the bloody and brawny chapters. The beheadings of the French Revolution will stir his imagination more than the lofty ideals of the Declaration of Independence. Expect a few discussions at the dinner table about the Indian scalpings or a choice execution. It will be told with all the adjectives necessary to spoil your appetite.

Teachers working with Arien children soon discover that Aries rarely sticks to one thing for too long. He gets little satisfaction from work well done, unless there is a prize involved. His satisfaction comes from novelty and competition. Once this passes, Arien interest stops. He may thoroughly enjoy the science experiment in class, but don't ask him to write a report on it once it's over. This, to Aries, is wasted effort.

The Arien child is likely to have many friends. He is fun to be with and has a certain aura of excitement about him. However, don't expect him to be warm and concerned about other children. He is much too wrapped up in himself. Don't bother reminding him of less fortunate children—he couldn't care less. He will collect for UNICEF at Halloween because it's fun. Don't expect many humanitarian motivations.

Sometimes, though, you may be surprised by apparent contradictions in the attitude of your Arien child. I remember recently a class discussion about the problem of starvation in Biafra. Mark, an 11-year-old, took a position at great variance with the other children.

"I don't see why we should worry about them," he said. "We have enough to worry about here. I think we should help our own people. But, still, we can't just let them die!"

I knew Mark was an Aries and it seemed a bit strange because ordinarily I would have expected him to be not at all interested in sharing the responsibility. So he wasn't acting according to his sign. But, then I checked his actual birthdate—it was March 23, at the very beginning of Aries with a strong Pisces influence. He was not a pure Arien, but a mixture of Pisces and Aries. The Pisces influence tended to make him more concerned with the problems of the world.

I could sense the struggle Mark was going through—torn between the two opposite notions. On the one hand, he felt he should be concerned—and on the other hand, he really was not. I found that my knowledge of his sun signs made it possible for me to understand the contradictory forces at work in Mark's character and to help him to ease the feelings of guilt this contradiction brought on.

Aries is usually very bright and finds studying easy. With encouragement and support, the Arien child can reach great heights with seemingly little effort. However, it is important for parents to remember that Aries will flit from one thing to another and this should not discourage them. The Arien youngster is the one who wants to play the piano today and the trumpet tomorrow. But once he has found a genuine challenge, look out! An Aries rarely knows defeat. Nothing is ever too difficult. The only problem is that it may become too boring.

Aries is likely to be the teacher's pet. Most teachers will respond to the Arien personality and zest for living. This is fine and Aries will love it. But be careful! If Aries doesn't like the teacher or finds her boring, then the poor teacher will be the object of pranks and persecution. Aries loves to poke fun!

The Arien child plays cat-and-mouse with teachers and school officials. He looks upon any confrontation with authority as a game to be won. In the principal's office, the Arien child will make any misdemeanor seem logical and natural, and will enjoy every minute of it! I have heard Arien children rationalize a playground fight into an unavoidable "accident" and turn an infraction of a rule into a moral course of action.

A good report card means nothing to Aries unless it represents some challenge. Aries will study to get ahead of the class brain but cares little for any philosophizing about good grades and getting ahead in life. Appealing to him in this way is a waste of words. Competition and challenge is the Arien motivation.

Arien children are bright, energetic, and fun to live with. They're full of excitement and vision. They're determined but not steadfast; interested but not devoted; challenged but not concerned.

You can expect a lot from your Arien child but only if you help him to live with his unbridled enthusiasm and love of change.

YOUR ARIES CHILD
   (MARCH 21–APRIL 20) MAY . . .
get his best grades in history
get good grades in geography and language
get only fair grades in mathematics and science
have some artistic ability
want to watch the more violent TV shows
be prone to hero-worship
blame others when he doesn't win a game or succeed
try to outdo and outshine his friends
listen to you attentively and then do exactly as he pleases
look forward to the first day of school

Your Aries Child (Pisces Side,
   March 21–April 5) May Also . . .
show very strong leanings toward the arts
tend to be moody and sensitive
be a charmer when he wishes
live in a world of phantasy
have nightmares and wild dreams
need constant reassurance
lean toward way-out fashion and grooming
cry, cry, cry

YOUR ARIES CHILD (TAURUS SIDE,
   APRIL 6–APRIL 20) MAY ALSO . . .
tend to be stubborn
love all outward signs of affection
balk at being pushed into the limelight
hate teasing
demand logical explanations for discipline
be able to perform vocal tricks—from singing to yodel-
   ing and shouting
draw well
react strongly to his environment, especially color

your child the

taurus

april 21–may 21
symbol:

the bull

ruling planet: **venus** • element: **earth**

POSITIVE CHARACTERISTICS:
Practicality, determination, kindness

NEGATIVE CHARACTERISTICS:
Overindulgence, materialism, stubbornness

IN HARMONY WITH:
Capricorn, Virgo, Cancer

> *Mary had a little lamb,*
> *Its fleece was white as snow,*
> *And everywhere that Mary went,*
> *The lamb was sure to go.*

And it had better—if it wants to reach sheephood.
Taurus Mary is very loyal but she demands loyalty in
return.

The Taurus is eternally loyal to his friends and equally ruthless to his enemies. His loyalty to people he likes is remarkable. Don't try to interfere with a Taurus child's friendships. You'll be asking for trouble. When you criticize a friend of Taurus, you criticize Taurus. He loves his possessions and these include his friends. He feels that certain people are his. He may single out one parent over another or one brother or sister over another. This will lead to family friction and should be discouraged as soon as you see it happening.

The Taurus is the plodder. No matter what his ability, he will keep on trying. The Taurus student burns the midnight oil and enjoys it. He is a determined individual and holds firm opinions. He knows what he believes and he believes that he is right. Once Taurus has decided on a plan of action, he will continue with it until he meets success. The Taurus child can wear out a teacher and exasperate a parent with his bull-like determination. He will do things over and over again until he does them right and they meet his satisfaction. Give him plenty of erasers when he sits down to do homework!

I remember Louise, a 13-year-old in my English class, who was a very careful worker. Frequently, when I corrected her papers, I would say: "You've made a slight error but don't bother to do it over."

But no matter how I would try to convince this Taurus child, I always knew that she would redo the whole paper anyway. It was not that she was such a perfectionist—it was just that she was determined to do a good job. It was almost as if she were interested in satisfying herself, rather than the teacher. Taurus children usually believe that they must do things the right way—and there is no alternative.

After a while I gave up trying to change Louise. After all,

it was part of her character and certainly would do no harm if not carried to extremes.

Another child—a youngster named Jamie—was in charge of the Christmas collection for a nearby orphanage. The whole school was busy gathering nickels and dimes.

Late on the last day of school—when the collection money was due to be turned over to me—I said to Taurus Jamie: "Don't bother to count the money—I'll do it, Jamie." But I should have known better. As a Taurus, it was inevitable that Jamie would count every last penny of the collection. Of course, that was exactly what Jamie did.

But if Taurus has determination, he is not quick to make a decision. He likes to mull things over and may be extremely slow in making up his mind. But, once something is decided, he sticks to it with steadfast conviction. This quality is especially true in his relationships with others.

Paradoxically, though determined students, Taurus children dread school as they do not learn easily. They dislike being called on in class and will rarely volunteer an answer, even when they know it. The teacher will probably complain that Taurus doesn't take part in class discussion. Yet, despite his silence in the classroom, he may amaze his teacher at examination time by getting a good grade. Taurus does well in examinations and tests but does poorly in daily recitation. He needs time to concentrate and think and dislikes being asked for a quick answer. He resents impromptu questioning or "pop" quizzes. His strong academic area will most likely be mathematics, especially if the problem deals with money. Taurus seems to have an instinctive understanding of money and finances. The Taurus child will handle his allowance very well and you can trust him to bring home the correct change from the store. He will probably save some of his allowance and amaze you with the amount he has managed to squirrel away.

The Taurus child is self-controlled and will rarely be found in the principal's office. He is quiet and unassuming. The only time he heads for trouble is when his patience has worn thin. When this happens, expect an unusual burst of temper. When Taurus loses his temper, it is really lost! He will tolerate a lot of abuse from parents, teachers, and other children before he does anything about it. He is the child who, when he throws a tantrum, elicits the remark, "It's just not like him!" He can take a great amount of pushing, but push him once too often and he'll turn on you.

An interesting thing about Taurus children is the delight they take in sensory pleasure. They love to smell a fragrant flower or a sweet perfume. They enjoy the taste of food and they like attractive clothing and decorated surroundings. The Taurus child will use some of mother's perfume or daddy's cologne. The Taurus girl loves to dress up in mother's finery. As a result of this intense interest in sensory pleasure, the Taurus child enjoys the arts and may show a definite artistic bent. Being able to blend their love of beauty with practicality, the Taurus child may well find a career in any phase of the arts.

The Taurus child is basically a stubborn child. His endurance is astounding and may well weaken your resistance. Frequently, when in opposition to you, he will say nothing, clench his teeth, and just stand there. When this happens, it is best to walk away and allow his stubborn nature to diminish in isolation. One of the best ways to appeal to him for cooperation is to offer a reward, especially a monetary one for a task well done. Holding out a practical goal he would like to achieve will motivate him.

A difficulty with Taurus children is their love of detail. When Taurus tells a story, be prepared for a description of every minor detail. When he does an arithmetic problem, he will labor over each step. This attention to detail can be extremely exasperating to a parent, especially when you help him with homework. Because of this penchant for detail, Taurus may not finish his school assignments on time. He may need help in budgeting his time and overcoming this scrupulous approach to assigned work. Help him to put first things first and to understand the value the rest of the world places on getting things done on time.

The Taurus child finds it easy to get in a rut and stay there. He may join the Scouts and discover that he hates it, yet refuse to give it up. A Taurus girl may refuse to wear her hair in another style or discard an old dress. Despite their warm and winning ways, many parents of Taurus children are constantly frustrated by their seemingly closed minds.

Taurus children are slow yet determined, loyal to the point of blind devotion, fond of sensory pleasure, preoccupied with money, and VERY, VERY, STUBBORN!

Your Taurus Child
   (April 21–May 21) May . . .
get his best grades in mathematics
get good grades in science
get only fair grades in social studies and language
amaze you with his determination and perseverance
be more a follower than a leader
do exactly as he is told
bore you with little details
love to eat
not actively participate in sports
be cautious with his allowance
be careless with his clothing

Your Taurus Child (Aries Side, April 21–May 5) May Also . . .

be very definite about everything, even if he has vague doubts

sometimes refuse to obey

tend to hurt himself easily

be openly affectionate

anger easily, but also forgive easily

forget what doesn't really matter deeply

have feelings hurt easily

accept everything as a challenge

start many projects but not finish many

learn easily

develop unevenly

show wild imagination

bounce back quickly

be very impatient

be a hero-worshipper

Your Taurus Child (Gemini Side,
   May 6–May 21) May Also . . .
be very curious
need constant activity
get bored easily
be noisy and very vocal
show signs of nervousness
have many enthusiasms
be friendly and outgoing
tend to be ambidextrous—good at any manual skill
exaggerate, color, lie a little
be short on persistence
seem to be moving in several directions at once
show signs of a quick wit
be tardy at school constantly
gab, gab, gab

♊

your child the

gemini

may 22–june 21
symbol:

the twins

ruling planet: **mercury** • element: **air**

~~~~~~

POSITIVE CHARACTERISTICS:
  Energy, wit, versatility

NEGATIVE CHARACTERISTICS:
  Flightiness, fickleness, restlessness

GETS ALONG BEST WITH:
  Aquarius, Libra

> *Ride a cockhorse to Banbury Cross,*
> *To see a fine lady upon a white horse;*
> *Rings on her fingers and bells on her toes,*
> *She shall have music wherever she goes.*

Well, Gemini loves an interesting detour!

The Gemini child should leave early for school or he'll be late—he has roving feet. Gemini will tell the teacher that he was late "because I watched a man fix his car," or, "I was following a dog I met along the way."

Gemini does not like to be held down and this certainly includes a daily school schedule. A little journey, no matter how short, gives Gemini a new lease on life. For this reason, a wise teacher will send the restless Gemini on some errand during the school day. A short trip to someplace out of the classroom will do more to calm the Gemini pupil than all the scolding in the world. If Gemini is held down too much, he may come to detest school, for he abhors rules and routine. The same is true at home. The less rules you give to Gemini, the better he will cooperate. Assigning him to take out the garbage will be less effective than asking him to do it every time.

The Gemini child usually learns quickly and easily and possesses an alert and active mind. He has a happy nature and a quick wit. Because of this, he may be a joy in the classroom under the guidance of a teacher who understands him. On the other hand, he could become the classroom dunce or clown. Parents of a Gemini will recognize this natural wit and cleverness. At times, it can brighten the household. At other times, it has to be controlled or it gets out of hand.

Sometimes your Gemini child needs to be handled with creative subtlety in order to make certain that he gets the most out of his education. Sixth-grader Peter was passing in all his subjects—but just passing. I noted that there were few things he really showed any interest in.

Then, one day, one of the teachers brought in an old clock she'd found in the attic. It wasn't working and she thought it might prove to be an interesting topic for discussion in class.

Peter perked up immediately. He asked if he could inspect it more carefully and in a few moments had taken the whole mechanism apart.

I asked him if he'd like to take it home and try to fix it, remembering that Geminis love to fix things because of their great manual dexterity. Peter was enthusiastic over the opportunity and next day he brought it back working perfectly. According to his parents, he had never taken apart a clock before!

So excited by this episode were his parents that they bought him a broken TV set and placed it in his bedroom. Within the week he had taken the whole mechanism apart and put it back together again. Unfortunately, it still didn't work.

But it was a lesson for Peter's parents—and for me. Geminis who show a lack of interest in their work can be steered into constructive, productive areas which suit their capabilities. As soon as Peter felt that his talents were being appreciated, he began doing better in his subjects as well. Self-esteem seems to be marvelously contagious.

If the Taurus child is determined to do a painstaking job, Gemini is the exact opposite. He just couldn't care less and finds it hard to complete an assignment. Chores at home are really chores to Gemini. It is often necessary to force them to finish what they begin, before they dash off on another tangent. Gemini is impatient and one of the difficult lessons he must learn is to follow a consistent course of action until his goal is attained.

Because of his alert, quick, receptive, and restless mentality, the Gemini child is the one who is more interested in what is going on outside the classroom than in what is happening inside the classroom. He is easily distracted and for this reason needs complete solitude in studying. Never allow a Gemini to study with a radio or TV. He just won't be able to do it. His powers of concentration are effective only without distraction. Frequently, a Gemini child recognizes this himself, and will develop little techniques to ensure solitude. Some will close their ears with their hands and others will even close their eyes tightly when they want to concentrate.

Gemini has a curious trait. He will use the same words and tokens of affection for all the people he loves. He will say the same thing to both Mom and Dad, and even to a favorite relative. Due to this, some people may think he's developing a line. He can shower his affection in all directions, being grandmother's darling, mother's darling, and daddy's darling. Obviously, this can backfire, and when it does, he can be accused of insincerity. Yet, Gemini is sure that he can love everybody without being disloyal to anybody. He can't understand why some people demand more affection.

This is likewise true with his friendships. You can expect your Gemini child to be the cause of some friction within his group. He tends to claim numerous best friends and will assure all his chums that they are his very *best* friends and companions. He means it, too!

The Gemini child also loves short cuts. He refuses to do anything the long way, if he knows an easier one. As a result, he will not always follow directions if he considers them a waste of effort.

"Why didn't you follow my directions?" will be answered with, "There was an easier way to do it!" This trait is a potential source of trouble with his teachers. The parent should help the Gemini to understand that there are certain established procedures to be followed. It will not be easy to teach, but it could save him from future difficulty.

Since the Gemini child is so attracted by every interesting thing that comes along, he will have to be taught to retain certain things of merit. Being prone to accept the new at the expense of the old is not always a virtue. There are certain tried and true ideas that should be cherished. For Gemini, retention is as difficult as concentration.

The Gemini child has great manual dexterity and enjoys fixing things. He has a fascination for gadgets and devices. He gets real enjoyment from using a new bottle opener or a clever mechanical toy. His toys and hobbies should explore this interest. Often, this may take a negative turn when he decides to take apart the new toy or fix his radio. Many a Christmas toy has not lasted the day at the hands of Gemini.

As the Gemini grows into maturity, it is important that he be given guidance in selecting a career. He is prone to changing his mind rather frequently. He may want to be a doctor today, a lawyer tomorrow and an engineer the next day. The ideal vocation will permit him to use his ingenuity to good advantage. The unhappy Gemini will be one who does the same thing day after day. As your Gemini girl matures, be prepared for a long series of boyfriends, and each one will be "the one." The Gemini adolescent will keep a parent frantic with new dates, new plans, and new activities.

No other sign of the Zodiac is so able to combine mental ingenuity with manual dexterity as does Gemini. Gemini could sell you the Brooklyn Bridge or blankets to an Indian. He is quick, witty, and agile. On the negative side, he tends to be nervous, restless, and too quick in making decisions. He has an alert mind and witty tongue that can be used to advantage or disadvantage.

The very best advice for parents of Gemini is to *guide* their child. The Gemini needs lots of help if he is to steer a steady course.

Your Gemini Child
(May 22–June 21) May . . .

get his best grades in language and reading
get good grades in mathematics and science
get only fair grades in history and geography
have an inventive mind
be late for dinner, for school, and for church
refuse to take a back seat to anyone
ignore the suggestions of others
write the pronoun "I" with a large letter
share with his playmate today and grab tomorrow
be indifferent to the problems of strangers
amaze you with his cleverness and initiative

Your Gemini Child (Taurus Side, May 22–June 6) May Also . . .

take over and organize everything in sight

be painfully frank sometimes

show signs of early maturity

tend to be very conservative

exhibit a furious temper

show signs of possessiveness

hide his real feelings

seem to be slow and plodding on the surface while hiding the real depth

be fantastically loyal to proven friends

freeze out anyone of whom he disapproves

find it hard to accept any criticism no matter how well-intended

YOUR GEMINI CHILD (CANCER SIDE,
  JUNE 6–JUNE 21) MAY ALSO . . .
have constantly changing moods
have very good memory
tend to need your approval and direction
be easily disciplined when young
become rebellious in adolescence
adopt imaginary playmates
cry easily
be sensitive to everyone's reaction to him
develop many fears and anxieties
never forget a birthday—his or yours
react to many problems by withdrawing himself
tend toward overeating or undereating
indulge in pixie-esque facemaking

your child the

cancer

(moonchild)
june 22–july 23
symbol:

the crab

ruling planet: **the moon** • element: **water**

POSITIVE CHARACTERISTICS:
Patience, persuasiveness, sensitivity
NEGATIVE CHARACTERISTICS:
Moodiness, self-pity, uncertainty
GETS ALONG BEST WITH:
Pisces, Scorpio, Taurus

Little Miss Muffet
Sat on a tuffet,
Eating some curds and whey.
Along came a spider,
And sat down beside her,
And frightened Miss Muffet away.

Little Miss Cancer Muffet simply must have security. And even that oh-so-social Aquarian spider is enough to set off her insecurities!

Yes, your moonchild or Cancer child is probably insecure, clinging, and domestic. He does not like being pushed out of the nest and will kick and scream when he encounters school for the first time. If this is not his reaction, then he will walk into kindergarten in a zombie-like state as though he were being led to the gallows. Following vacations and holidays there may even be tears and hesitation about returning to school. This sometimes manifests itself all the way up to college. If anyone comes home over the weekend, it will be Cancer.

There was a little fellow in the kindergarten class of my school who cried constantly.

Now, it's normal for a child to cry the first days—but after a month of crying, something has to be done. The teacher simply could not stop him. Little Alfie would come into the room quietly, sit in a corner, and cry the whole day.

The teacher came to my office and said: "You've got to do something. Either his parents must withdraw him and keep him home for an extra year or we've got to find a way to stop that crying. I can't stand it anymore."

So after a chat with his mother by telephone, I went down to the classroom and invited Alfie up to my office. I had his permanent record folder with all the information about him, including his birthday. I noted that his birthday was in early July. A Cancer, like myself. Instinctively, I knew how to handle it.

"Alfie," I said, "when I was your age and my parents sent me to school I was sure that it was because they were tired of me and didn't really love me. But, you know, I found out that wasn't true at all!"

Suddenly, Alfie was listening, although still sobbing.

"Just to make sure about your mother and father, I called your Mom on the telephone this morning and she assured me that they really do love you very, very much."

Alfie listened solemnly and gradually stopped crying. I took him by the hand and led him back to the classroom where the amazed teacher flashed me a look of supreme gratitude.

Next day, Alfie's mother told me that when he had arrived home she asked him how school went that day. He smiled and told her all about the class activities.

"And, Mommy," he said, "I know that you and Daddy really love me!"

"How do you know that?" his mother asked.

"Because the President told me in his office," Alfie said.

It was the easiest promotion in my entire academic career.

During those first crucial days of school, the wise parent will try to make it a special and less disturbing time. Perhaps you could prepare a special after-school treat or plan a special evening entertainment. And a word of warning—don't try to send a Cancer off to summer camp without a lot of preparation. It just won't work and you'll end up by bringing him home!

Cancer does not react too well to harshness or punishment. He needs the feeling of support and comfort from those he loves or he may become despondent and dejected. If poorly handled by an unsympathetic teacher, Cancer could hate school with an unbridled passion.

The Cancerian child is moody. His sign is ruled by the Moon and his moods change like the Moon. At one moment, he is happy and carefree. Without warning, he becomes somber and full of self-pity. Never try to figure out Cancer's moods—just learn to live with them. Remember that no mood will last too long.

Nevertheless, on the whole, the Cancerian child is happy and relaxed. His greatest liability is his extreme sensitivity. The slightest rebuke from teacher or parent will upset him and convince him that nobody loves him. He cannot tolerate criticism of any kind and tends to be a poor loser. When you play games with a Cancerian child, be certain he wins. If not, get ready for some unpleasantness. He associates losing with rejection.

Cancer is capable of intense love and devotion. Because of this, he is usually a mamma's boy or daddy's little darling. This parental devotion carries certain dangers. A possessive mother or father will have little difficulty in binding the Cancerian child with a burdensome silver cord. The prudent parent will allow Cancer a freedom of affection and guard against an unhealthy dependency.

The Cancerian youngster is highly artistic. He loves color and decoration. Give him lots of coloring books and perhaps a tin of water colors. Shades and hues fascinate him and he will often be lured by color. He will select an ice cream flavor more by color than taste.

Cancer also loves to dress up, especially in some exotic fashion. Halloween is likely to be his favorite holiday (next to Christmas, which is traditionally a family day). He probably decorates his room with his belongings. The Cancerian boy may hang pennants or photographs and the Cancerian girl may decorate with stuffed animals and dolls. She is a natural mother-type and he is a natural father-type. And don't be too surprised if the Cancerian boy plays house once in a while.

Being tidy and meticulous are other Cancerian traits. However, Cancers may be more careful of their surroundings than of themselves. They may be disheveled but their drawers are neatly arranged.

Cancer is sensitive in the positive meaning of the term. He possesses a kind of sixth sense that tells him what people want. For this reason, the Cancerian student can please his teacher easily and might become the teacher's pet.

Eventually, the Cancerian child will reveal his tendency toward procrastination. He likes to put things off and dislikes being asked for a quick decision. He likes to think things over before deciding on a plan of action. Due to this, he is a born businessman. He can investigate all angles and instinctively know what to do. Without comprehending it himself, he knows people, and he knows how to handle them.

Cancer accumulates. It's the Cancerian child who will have the stamp collection, the rock collection, or just a collection. His drawers and toy box will always be full of treasures. If you should suggest disposing of anything, it will be met with wails of protest. His pack-rat nature inclines him to hoard.

One of Cancer's great luxuries is to allow himself to become so depressed that he loses sight of reality. Despite any contrary arguments or pleading, the Cancerian child may decide that school is intolerable or that he has no friends. He will brood and feel terribly sorry for himself. Or he may have flights of fancy and decide that his real parents put him out for adoption and you won't tell him the truth for fear of hurting him. At times like these, it is best to humor Cancer. Try kidding him out of his dark moods, but, for goodness sake, DON'T commiserate!

The Cancerian child is warm and sympathetic. People usually like him and enjoy his company. He radiates a feeling of compassion and concern and people seem to trust him. He enjoys his home and is happiest at home. Parents of Cancer never need worry that Cancer will stray too far away. He is so comfortable at home that he can play alone for hours on end and have as good a time as if he were with a hundred playmates.

If you can teach your Cancer child to be less moody, less indecisive, and less inclined to make mountains out of molehills, his life will be more pleasant. And so will yours!

Your Cancer Child
(June 22–July 23) May . . .
get his best grades in language arts
get good grades in health, music, and art
get only fair grades in mathematics
shun his friends periodically
be overly dramatic
often pretend some great injury or misfortune
have a vivid imagination
be "mother's little baby"
treasure the past
be extremely patient with friends and playmates
be tender with animals

Your Cancer Child (Gemini Side,
  June 22–July 6) May Also . . .
be brilliant and original
be impatient with slower movers and thinkers
have difficulty in making choices
show a tendency to vacillate
be subject to deep depressions
be the life of the party at times, too
often show irritability
have talent for languages
be interested and active in the arts
take advice badly
lie easily
tend to drop plans if they show signs of problems

YOUR CANCER CHILD (LEO SIDE,
  JULY 7–JULY 23) MAY ALSO . . .

insist on his own way and sulk when stymied
be a natural leader
boss other children—and you, if you allow it
show off
be very proud and dignified
enjoy people fussing over him
intersperse activity with periods of laziness
*be pushy and outgoing (but this may not be obvious
  in youth)*
be a bit on the vain side
compete with his instructors
be a good student if encouraged, lousy if ignored
be extravagant
*be a party-party type with great interest in opposite
  sex*
need constant affection and signs of faith

your child the
leo
july 24–august 23
symbol:
the lion
ruling planet: **the sun** • element: **fire**

POSITIVE CHARACTERISTICS:
Pride, self-assurance, generosity

NEGATIVE CHARACTERISTICS:
Arrogance, egotism, authoritarianism

GETS ALONG BEST WITH:
Sagittarius, Aries

Old King Cole
Was a merry old soul,
And a merry old soul was he.
He called for his pipe,
And he called for his bowl,
And he called for his fiddlers three.

Leo is King—and he wants you to know it!

67

Leo has enormous pride and haughtiness. He thinks in terms of I and mine. These are his key words. Leo is self-centered and egotistical. He needs help in understanding this tendency and in controlling it. This egocentricity can be put to good use, but it will take effort and lots of self-control.

The Leonian child, with his aggressive qualities, is likely to roar like a lion when he is crossed. This is another trouble spot. When angered, he is certain that he is right and finds it very difficult to back down.

The Leonian child is one of the most generous and noble children of the Zodiac. He can hardly wait for school to begin each September because he enjoys being with other children and relishes the challenge of learning new things. He is keenly competitive and shows it in his schoolwork. He rarely shies away from a difficult task and thoroughly enjoys demonstrating his ability. Leo is a born showman and loves to perform whether it be for company, on the playing field, or in the classroom. The Leonian child is a true extrovert and a born leader. He is the youngster who takes command of a situation, leads the team, or organizes the game. Teachers and parents would be wise to channel this quality into some constructive expression. Unchecked, it could cause problems.

In the good old days when there were dress codes, 16-year-old Debbie came to school over-dressed and over-made-up. Everyday was prom day for Debbie and she was reported to the office for violating the dress code.

In talking with her, she made it clear that she didn't feel that she was violating the dress code. She felt that she was always in very good taste. Debbie even looked down her nose at the dress of her classmates. They were the ones who were out of step!

In typical Leo fashion, she sneered at the issue being made over her fine clothing, suspecting that the other girls were jealous and that she was being victimized for her good taste.

There comes a time, particularly with a strong personality, where you must simply lay down the rules and insist that they be followed to the letter, and accept no compromise. I did that.

Debbie agreed to comply, but under protest. I suggested that if she really felt so strongly, she use those energies in fighting to change the dress codes so that her own ideas would be acceptable.

"Change them!" she said. "I want to do away with them."

Maybe she's won!

Leo's personality is warm and magnetic and draws others to it. He is self-assured and can be exceedingly generous. He needs love and needs to give love. The Leonian child will have a favorite parent and usually one best friend. He cannot spread his affection around. He is the one-man type. You will find that Leonian children have favorite teachers, too. Strangely enough, these teachers will more than likely be the strict ones—the stricter the better. Leo admires strength and firm control. Let this guide you in handling your Leonian child.

Never let him see your weakness or your inability to handle a situation. Leo will step right in and take charge if he feels you are not capable. If this happens, you may find the child making decisions for the parent. Leo will tell you what to buy for dinner, what clothing to buy, and when he should go to bed. One Leonian child I know has so bullied his parents that he literally runs the household.

In school, Leo needs praise and an incentive to achieve. Whatever your Leo's interests are, encourage him and he will please you with his effort. Leo can be a real success and a source of great parental pride if he gets sufficient encouragement.

The Leonian child sets high standards for himself and, as a result, wants the best things in life. He enjoys fine clothing and expensive toys. He craves a feeling of well-being and comfort. This desire for material satisfaction sometimes inclines Leo toward laziness. At times, he may prefer to sit down and loaf when he should be working. A little prodding will usually move him on.

Being a strong sign, Leo likes to step in to help others or try to run the lives of others. When this happens, he seems to forget that some people might resent his intrusion. The Leonian child is frequently told to mind his own business by his playmates. When told this, he cannot understand why it was said. The Leonian child finds it hard to comprehend this seeming pettiness in others. His usual retort is, "But I was just trying to help."

Your Leonian child always goes forward. He will rarely look back. To him, the past is gone and forgotten. Never remind him of a past mistake as a guide for future action. Leo is only concerned with what is ahead. To remind him that he didn't enjoy camping last summer will have no effect on his desire to camp this summer. He couldn't care less!

The prudent parent will encourage Leo to participate in sports or to assume positions of responsibility. The team captain or the Student Council president are tailor-made positions for the Leo. More than any other sign, Leo thinks big and will welcome any opportunity to demonstrate his leadership.

The Leonian child's sign is masculine in nature and Leonian girls will show some typically masculine traits. They may be aggressive, good at sports, domineering, and authoritative. These can be positive qualities if carefully used but could be disastrous on a date.

Leo never wants to be in a subordinate position. He craves power and authority. For this reason, he may resent the new babysitter or the new teacher. He is most willing to be controlled if he recognizes superior strength, but he will test a novice. Should the new babysitter and the new teacher show any timidity, the Leonian child will pounce on them.

During play, the Leonian child can be haughty, domineering, and imperious. He will boss the other children and this can spell trouble. Help him to use his leadership abilities wisely. If your Leonian child is shunned by other children for a while, it is probably his own fault.

Leonian youngsters can be warm, energetic, and magnetic. They have quick minds and enjoy competition and challenge. With encouragement, they can do anything they want to do. They need to exercise prudent self-control in dealing with other people, since they want to dominate. Since they think in terms of I instead of We, they are sure that their every motive is right and just.

Like the lion, your own Leo can be roaring, regal, and fearsome. But handle him gently, and you'll have him purring like a kitten.

Your Leo Child
      (July 24–August 23) May . . .
do his best in physical education
get good grades in language and reading
get only fair grades in science
disturb you with his favoritism
have periodic fits of laziness
assume airs of self-importance
go into occasional moods of despondency
be generous with others
let you know full well when he is displeased
trust his friends and favorites

YOUR LEO CHILD (CANCER SIDE,
 JULY 24–AUGUST 7) MAY ALSO . . .
try to avoid any physical violence
finish every job begun
be warm and kind towards intimates
show great patience
be easily hurt
tend to withdraw if he senses disapproval
be secretive when hurt
criticize and nag
never forget an insult
feel nothing is ever completely right
spot phoniness immediately
love the family
love antiques, stamps, etc.—anything old, including
 you
be open and above board

YOUR LEO CHILD (VIRGO SIDE,
   AUGUST 8–AUGUST 23) MAY ALSO . . .
be a born mimic
be a very picky eater
be outgoing in the family, shy among strangers
be neat and careful about belongings
be easily disciplined
worry himself sick sometimes
be embarrassed by public criticism
prove a great help to mother and teacher
accept responsibility for chores
be shy with the opposite sex
sometimes be too frank
demand tidiness and efficiency in others
insist on privacy
understand other people's problems
be very down-to-earth

your child the

virgo

august 24–september 23
symbol:

the virgin

ruling planet: **mercury** • element: **earth**

POSITIVE CHARACTERISTICS:
Industry, sympathy, intelligence

NEGATIVE CHARACTERISTICS:
Pettiness, irritability, bias

GETS ALONG BEST WITH:
Capricorn, Taurus

Humpty Dumpty sat on a wall,
Humpty Dumpty had a great fall;
All the king's horses
And all the king's men
Couldn't put Humpty Dumpty together again.

Not well enough to please perfectionist Virgo, anyway!

The Virgo child is apt to be hypercritical. Being a perfectionist, he finds it hard to tolerate shortcomings in others. The teacher or Scout leader of a Virgo is open to much criticism. Don't take these complaints too seriously. As far as Virgo is concerned, they never do anything right!

Virgo is a born student. The Virgo child accepts school as a natural situation and is quite comfortable in the classroom. He studies diligently and has a good memory. Virgo is the youngster who studies during recess and who carries extra books home at night. You will rarely have to push a Virgo into doing his homework.

However, sometimes he can be very critical of an educational system which he believes is failing to accomplish its purpose.

For instance, a friend who is a high school teacher asked me for advice on handling a 16-year-old student activist in his homeroom. Virgo Larry had posted a sign on the bulletin board objecting to the lack of relevancy of Ancient History. When brought to the office, Larry protested the stupidity of an educational system which teaches youngsters about the glories of ancient Rome while our own civilization is being destroyed.

"I don't want to know about things which happened thousands of years ago. . . . I want to know what's happening now!" he shouted. Larry claimed he was fighting the battle not for himself, but for the students who would follow in the future.

I asked my friend why Larry had to study Ancient History.

"I'll tell you why," my friend said with annoyance. "Because I had to! Why should that little son-of-a-gun get away with it!"

He was joking, of course. And we discussed the best way to handle the situation with an analytical Virgo. Obviously, the argument that ancient history is merely preparation for current history was a good one. History as a biography of the present is something a Virgo would understand. The totality of a course of study, the need for an understanding of the whole civilized world—these were the arguments to put forth, it was agreed.

My friend went back to his school and faced Larry with these solid arguments. Larry canceled his anti-Ancient History rally.

Next term, though, Larry is scheduled to take Solid Geometry. Try that one for relevancy!

Virgo is a very conscientious sign with a tremendous amount of patience. Time does not disturb the Virgo and, as a result, he is better able to handle difficult or tedious situations than any other sun sign. This, together with Virgo's fine mind and analytical ability, makes for an ideal student. More than any other sign, Virgo has a positive genius for analyzing and breaking something down into its component parts. It is a logical and rational sign with a passion for accuracy.

The Virgo child's bookbag is likely to be stuffed with notes and memoranda, and he probably keeps records of things that have happened. The Virgo girl may keep a diary.

Very little misses Virgo's keen eye. He observes everything and remembers it. If there is a spot on your dress, your Virgo will notice it—and never promise him something you cannot deliver. Virgo always remembers and sees to it that you don't forget!

The Virgo nature is exceedingly conscientious and imbued with a desire to be of service to others. Your Virgo child will accept household chores with little or no resistance. Taking out the trash or making the bed will be done without a reminder and it will be done well. Virgo girls are natural babysitters and take the responsibility seriously. Whether it be a paper route, lawn work, or babysitting, the Virgo child will do it well.

A virtue of the Virgo that we might all envy is his ability to save for a rainy day. The Virgo child will usually save some of his allowance and is never without a nickel or a dime. He loves to save and practice thrift. Notice how Virgo cares for his toys.

One difficulty with a Virgo child is his tendency to become wrapped up in details. Keeping everything neat and tidy, keeping records, meeting assignments, and being generally helpful may prevent him from considering the large-scale goals. The Virgo student may be so busy studying that he never takes time to think about a vocational choice. This procrastination with the larger problems of life may disturb others. The parents of a Virgo should help the youngster understand that there are larger problems to be considered. The Virgo sometimes can't see the forest for the trees.

Since the Virgo characteristics are those of a conservative person, expect this thinking to develop in your child. He is usually not a follower and cares little about what his peers are doing. He is, in fact, more prone to accept the standards of the adult community and regard his friends as silly and stupid. With this maturity of views, he is likely to be very critical of his peers and they may resent his opposition. It is not the Virgo who adopts the current fad or insists on wearing the in clothing.

Virgo youngsters, especially the girls, are chatty and tend to gossip. Being analytical, Virgo loves to gather the facts about others and speculate about relationships. He is always trying to figure out other people, and may even appear suspicious of their motives. Virgo is the child who is curious about who loves whom among his friends or tries to pry into his teacher's private life. It would be wise to curb this dangerous use of one of Virgo's gifts should you notice it developing in your child. Teach him to respect other people's privacy.

Your Virgo child may not be a warm, loving child. Some astrologers attribute a certain coldness to this sign. The Virgo may give freely of his time and energy but he does not give freely of his emotions. Your Virgo child may not cry too easily and may seem unmoved by your show of affection. These are the children who pull away from the embrace of a visiting aunt or uncle.

Virgo girls are often skilled in some kind of handiwork. Mothers will find it easy to teach them knitting or embroidery. Virgo has an inherent sense of good taste and this is especially obvious in the girl. The Virgo girl is meticulous and careful in her dress and parents will seldom have to criticize either her choice or care of clothing.

Chances are your Virgo child is bright, analytical, and conscientious. He is probably a born student, mindful of his school assignment. He is ruled by the notion of "doing for others," yet he can be extremely critical of others. Virgo can become burdened with details and must guard against this shortcoming. If any Virgo child experiences difficulty in school, this will more than likely be the cause.

Virgo is also prone to drive himself beyond endurance. As this could damage his health, it is a Virgo trait to guard against. You must let him know when enough is enough!

YOUR VIRGO CHILD
    (AUGUST 24–SEPTEMBER 23) MAY . . .
get his best grades in social studies
get good grades in mathematics, science, and health
get only fair grades in artistic pursuits
sometimes seem impossible to please
have very little laziness about him
make a poor patient when sick in bed
become upset by sudden and unexpected setbacks
be among the very first to discover the scratch you got
   on the new car
be a fussy eater
be overly concerned with cleanliness

YOUR VIRGO CHILD (LEO SIDE,
   AUGUST 24–SEPTEMBER 7) MAY ALSO . . .
be proud and haughty
prove to be a born leader
be very generous, give away toys, and so forth
tend to be a bit timid under much bluster
play hunches
react positively to flattery
be on the flamboyant side
not maliciously cause hurt in others
tend to generalize and make sweeping assumptions
be amazed that anybody wants to get the best of him
sulk when crossed
be lovable when loved, hateful when hated

YOUR VIRGO CHILD (LIBRA SIDE,
    SEPTEMBER 8–SEPTEMBER 23) MAY ALSO . . .
be physically attractive
be unnerved by decision-making
hate to be rushed
react best to firm but subtle direction
be very sensitive to other people's feelings
need calm, beautiful surroundings
alternate periods of activity and periods of recharging
have winning gentle ways
be good on the debating team
keep secrets
tend to overweight
be constantly napping
have weekly crushes

your child the
libra
september 24–october 23
symbol:
the scales
ruling planet: **venus** • element: **air**

POSITIVE CHARACTERISTICS:
Alertness, diplomacy, charm

NEGATIVE CHARACTERISTICS:
Indolence, vanity, escapism

GETS ALONG BEST WITH:
Aquarius, Gemini

> *A-hunting we will go,*
> *A-hunting we will go.*
> *Catch a fox,*
> *Put him in a box,*
> *Then we'll let him go.*

Luck for the fox that Libra made the plans. Librans like everything arranged in an exact way and any change in plan upsets them.

83

Libran children have very little patience with readjustment. Whenever you plan a party or a picnic with your Libran youngster, a change or alteration in plans will bring tears of protest. The more sudden the change, the louder the Libran protest. It is wise to prepare a Libran for any possible change of plans well ahead of time and allow him to anticipate the possibility.

Libran children have a particular warmth and a charming manner. Their main interest in school is social. They are excellent students and possess a keen imagination but what they learn out of school is often more important than what they learn in school.

The Libran child likes all the good things of life. One of his greatest joys is music and many will express a desire to play an instrument. Music lessons are seldom wasted on a Libran. Art lessons, too, will prove a present joy and, possibly, good preparation for a future career.

Several years ago, my wife and I were hosts to a 10-year-old Herald-Tribune Fresh Air Fund child from the Brownsville section of Brooklyn. It was our first experience with an underprivileged youngster and we expected a child who would reflect his harsh background. We'd heard awesome stories and we were a bit apprehensive.

Instead, we got one of the most sensitive youngsters I'd ever met. Deprived of any cultural enrichment, his artistic yearnings were searching for an outlet.

Once when we visited a friend, our guest went immediately to the piano where he fondled the keys and finally dared to try out some sounds. When it was time to go, we had to pull him away. He was sad and moody, as if he had seen a world in which he could never partake.

On a rainy day, we gave him a water color set and paper and showed him how to use them. To our amazement, the boy had an innate talent and a keen sense of color and form.

84

By the time he left, this Libra child was really opening up.

When we sent him back, we felt guilty because he was returning to a tenement where he could not pursue his artistic talents. So, we made plans to sponsor his piano lessons and we sent a supply of art materials as a Christmas present.

Every summer for three years, we had him back, took him to museums, introduced him to all the arts. Now he is a young man, launching himself in a successful art career, proof that the artistic direction of a Libra will always manage to find an outlet somehow.

A Libran will think out all the possibilities and then try to manipulate everyone accordingly. When he does this and turns on his charm to its fullest, mother, dad, aunts, and uncles will all fall into line. This Libran magnetism and determination will be of equal advantage in the classroom. If Libran effort does not get passing grades, then Libran charm will. Many a teacher has been an unknowing victim of this calculated aim to please.

Libran children are very often creative and should do well in the arts. However, expect no abstract art from this sign. Their artistic expression is likely to be very precise and correct. A Libran draws a house that looks like a house and a cow that looks like a cow. The artistic interpretation will be highly realistic. This is why the precision and mathematical structure of music hold such great appeal for this sign, and why so many great musicians were born under this sun sign. Among musical Librans are Horowitz, Franz Liszt, Shostakovich, and George Gershwin.

This is a very time-conscious sign. The Libran child asks, "How many days until my birthday?" or, "How many days until Christmas?" He will probably learn to tell time earlier than most children. Among his first requests may be the desire to own a watch. He is rarely tardy and is quite disturbed when others are late. He puts value on punctuality, not only

85

for himself but for others as well. He may complain that the Scout meeting did not start on time or that the teacher did not start class on time. And when you tell him that dinner will be at six, expect to see him sitting at the table awaiting you.

One of the Libran special talents is the ability to make something attractive and beautiful out of the ordinary and common. The Libran has great ingenuity and an innate cleverness. The report done by a Libran child at school may not be scholarly or very long, but it will be neat and bound in an attractive cover. This alone may sometimes win a passing grade. Frequently, Libra is more concerned with the pretty cover than with the work inside. He is equally as concerned about his clothing and has a firm sense of good taste about apparel. He has a good color sense and always looks well put together. His room will reflect his passion for neatness and you will not have to remind the Libran child to tidy up his room or hang up his clothing.

Another Libran virtue is politeness. The Libran youngster is usually a courteous youngster. It is not too difficult to teach him good manners. "Thank you," and "You're welcome," come easily to him. You can capitalize on this by teaching good manners early. Once taught, you will never have to remind Libra what he has learned and he will make you proud in public. "What a polite little child," is a frequent comment made of Librans.

A difficulty with the Libran youngster is his tendency to keep plans and ambitions from you. He can be very tight-lipped and there will be times when you will not know what he is thinking. He is especially secretive about those things that he holds vital to happiness and success. Help him to confide in you and to trust your interest in his ambitions. And when Libra does confide in you, always respect that confidence or he'll never open up again.

The Libran child is usually surrounded by relatives—his magnetism draws them to him. Aunts and uncles, grandparents and cousins will shower him with attention and gifts. There is some danger that the Libran child will use these people. This must be guarded against should you see any indication that it is happening. Sometimes the Libran may turn to a grandmother or grandfather to indulge some whim denied him by you. He may even do it without your knowledge. Librans often suggest Christmas presents far in advance of the holiday!

Your Libran child probably has a magnetic personality. He is precise and methodical and desires a well-ordered life. He can be possessive of you and usually demands your complete attention. This carries over into school in his relationships with teachers. He can be just as demanding in the classroom. Although bright, the Libran is not often a good student. As observed, he is apt to play the angles rather than study. However, he will probably do it with skill and subsequent success.

Parental relationships are very important to the Libran. He tends to be overly possessive of his parents and demands much love and attention. Any intrusion from a new baby brother or sister may stir up feelings of intense proportions. One Libran child was so upset over the adoption of a new brother that the parents had to return the child to the adoption agency. Librans make devoted sons and daughters but they must be taught that love is to be shared.

In your old age, it is your Libran child who will assure your comfort and security.

YOUR LIBRA CHILD
   (SEPTEMBER 24—OCTOBER 23) MAY . . .
get his best grades in artistic subjects
get good grades in any form of expressive language
get only fair grades in history and geography
have musical or other artistic talents
have a short memory for obligations
waste time splitting hairs
be physically attractive
be overly concerned with fairness
resent new family members
remind you of your promises
be affectionate

YOUR LIBRA CHILD (VIRGO SIDE,
  SEPTEMBER 24–OCTOBER 8) MAY ALSO . . .
be very practical
be very sure of himself
*maintain strict standards and expect other people to
  live up to them, too*
be too much of a perfectionist
*if there's a choice between intellect and emotion—
  choose intellect*
be dependable and hard working
be very prompt
have a dry humor
tend to be concise to the point of abruptness
hate phoney and pompous people
object to crudeness
be very big on self-improvement programs

YOUR LIBRA CHILD (SCORPIO SIDE,
   OCTOBER 9–OCTOBER 23) MAY ALSO . . .

be physically strong

be strong-willed as well

want to win and be willing to fight long and hard for it

be a bad loser

tend to trample on the weak

admire strength in others

show a great need for privacy

make sarcastic comments

place a lock on his diary

be good at hiding things—and finding things as well

withstand pain well

reveal a sometimes uncontrollable anger

be fantastically loyal and demand loyalty in return

be curious to the extent of being nosy

have enormous energy that needs to be channeled

be a lover-boy but detest infidelity

need to be taught love—and then can return it

end up at the top of whatever he chooses

your child the

scorpio
october 24–november 22
symbol:
the scorpion
ruling planet: **mars** • element: **water**

POSITIVE CHARACTERISTICS:
Passion, determination, independence

NEGATIVE CHARACTERISTICS:
Sarcasm, vindictiveness, dominance

GETS ALONG BEST WITH:
Cancer, Pisces

Oh, where have you been,
Billy boy, Billy boy?
Oh, where have you been,
Charming Billy?

On a secret Scorpio mission, no doubt! If there's one thing a Scorpio likes better than mere privacy—it's mysterious secrecy.

Scorpio is one of the most invincible signs of the Zodiac. He makes up his mind quickly and then carries out his plan with determination. He is a strategist and leaves nothing to chance, studying the entire picture and anticipating every possible consequence. He has a brilliance and depth of mind that is to be envied. The Scorpio child will ask his teacher questions that might embarrass an Einstein.

However, a problem with Scorpio is his disregard for anything that does not interest him. A Scorpio child couldn't care less about the way the Indians built their teepees or how bees collect honey. Unless he has committed himself to be interested, he literally turns off. Obviously, this can cause some problems in school.

The Scorpio likes the excitement of a science experiment or building a puppet theater but he has disdain for the nitty-gritty of basic skills. He likes to read, but he will probably hate reading lessons. He doesn't care about word skills—he just wants to read the story.

Scorpio has a gift for concentration and, once his attention is engaged, he is relentless in pursuing it. Like a detective, he wants to know what's going on and why. Scorpio prods and snoops and can make himself slightly unwelcome. The Scorpio child keeps asking questions and the answers never seem to satisfy him. Your Scorpio child may like to go through your drawers or snoop in your purse.

The Scorpio youngster is quite willing to accept responsibility. He seems to realize instinctively that life has problems to be met and solved.

Scorpios sometimes accept situations that others bemoan and turn them to their advantage. The Scorpio child will probably have an after-school job and will get it by himself.

One of Scorpio's most interesting facets is his ability to uncover things that might remain hidden to others. You can't hide much from a Scorpio for too long. He will find the Christmas presents long before Christmas and he will know all the family secrets. Remember this if your motives for telling your Scorpio child anything are untrue.

The Scorpio child loves nature and enjoys partaking of it. He likes to take walks in the woods and be off by himself. The little Scorpio girl likes nothing better than searching for wildflowers or picking berries. The Scorpio boy will more than likely show an interest in hunting, fishing, and camping. These outdoor activities give the Scorpio a chance to be alone. He needs occasional periods of solitude to recharge his batteries. Make certain that you provide these for your Scorpio. You and he will be much happier if you do!

Scorpio loves to play cat and mouse. He sees a confrontation with others as a game and derives enjoyment out of baiting others. The Scorpio child likes to tease and taunt, even to the point of bringing other children to tears. You should help your Scorpio to avoid this abuse of his cleverness.

One of the most fascinating characteristics of many Scorpio's is the expression in their eyes. There is a penetrating yet remote quality that can disturb people. Notice this expression develop in your Scorpio youngster and teach him to use it wisely.

You will find that Scorpio can be trusted and can keep a secret. If you tell a Scorpio child not to tell, he won't! His lips are sealed. On the other hand, don't expect the Scorpio to tell you any of his secrets. He does not confide in others but keeps things to himself. You will find that your Scorpio child will not reveal his true feelings. He prefers to remain aloof and introspective.

Scorpio is not especially gregarious. In fact, he tends to be slightly introverted. He is not the life of the party and may even refuse to attend the party! In a roomful of people, the

Scorpio can sit quietly and rarely speak, yet his presence is always felt. Some people claim that Scorpio can communicate without words! He can transmit his approval or disapproval just by thnking it. Notice how often you will seem to read his mind and anticipate his answers.

A shortcoming of this magnetic sign is the tendency to hold a grudge. The Scorpio finds it hard to forgive and even harder to forget. When Scorpio has a disagreement with a playmate, it may grow into a permanent feud. His determined nature refuses to let bygones be bygones. You will often find yourself urging him to forgive his friends or his brothers and sisters. Another Scorpio problem is his suspicious nature. He never accepts things on face value and demands proof before he will accept. In this regard, he can be a real challenge to his teachers.

Scorpio is a magnetic and dynamic sign. The Scorpio is resourceful and energetic and can be a joy or a terror, depending on how he uses his gifts. He tends to withdraw and be a loner, yet he can exert a tremendous hold over others without even trying. He gives his attention only to that which interests him and then may become too wrapped up in it. He is nagged by the fear that others will surpass him although he may never admit to it.

As a school board member, I am aware of the increasing problem of teenage pregnancy in high school. If what astrologers say is true—that Scorpio is a lusty sign—teachers specializing in mid-wifery had better look to the Scorpio student. Not only might she be the first one pregnant, but secretly pregnant! But how long can that be a secret?

I remember one case of an unwed Scorpio mother-to-be who knew just what she wanted. She made no bones about the fact that a home and family were it. Although parents and friends proposed several acceptable and unacceptable solutions, this girl and the father of her unborn child knew they wanted to be married. And that is exactly what happened in true Scorpio fashion.

With Scorpio's determination and today's easy morality, parents of Scorpio children had better be wary, or be prepared for early babysitting chores.

Your Scorpio Child
(October 24–November 22) May . . .
do his best in mathematics and science
do well in physical education and health
get only fair grades in the social sciences
have some inclination toward self-indulgence
make a faithful friend and a bitter enemy
be somewhat conservative in his thinking
tend toward some bad personal habits
have a fascination for disease and medical treatment
have a certain immobility of facial expression
exert a will of iron

YOUR SCORPIO CHILD (LIBRA SIDE,
    OCTOBER 24–NOVEMBER 8) MAY ALSO . . .

need beauty and luxury
be upset by ugliness and violence
tend to act as mediator
be fair to the point of cruelty to those he loves
need praise and adulation
be hypersensitive
want peace at any price
possess great beauty and charm
show exquisite taste in clothing
try to become involved in arts
sometimes show a false front

Your Scorpio Child (Sagittarius Side,
  November 9–November 22) May Also . . .
have a terrible fear of rejection
need people desperately
always remain a child at heart
seem to be happy-go-lucky
be brutally honest
demand logical answers
constantly ask WHY?-WHY?-WHY?
detest hypocrisy
tend to be clumsy
need to feel free
have no feeling for money
love learning if it's not made too dry
drop out
show an interest in religion

your child the

sagittarius
november 23–december 21
symbol:
the archer
ruling planet: **jupiter** • element: **fire**

POSITIVE CHARACTERISTICS:
Determination, curiosity, inventiveness

NEGATIVE CHARACTERISTICS:
Flightiness, impatience, impulsiveness

GETS ALONG BEST WITH:
Aries, Leo, other Sagittarians

Polly, put the kettle on,
Polly, put the kettle on,
Polly, put the kettle on,
We'll all have tea.

"Not me!" says Sagittarius Polly.

The phrase that typifies the Sagittarian youngster is: "Nobody's going to tell me what to do!" Sagittarius is an independent soul and inclined to resent authority. You can expect some trouble in school from your Sagittarian and he may develop into a genuine discipline problem. You must start early in helping him to understand and control his independent spirit.

Sagittarian boys and girls may develop stomach aches or dizzy spells in school as a reaction against classroom control. They simply do not like the confinement of the classroom, and the threat of staying after school is the cruelest punishment the teacher could suggest. Because of their dislike for school, you will find that your Sagittarian responds best to the easy, relaxed teacher. A strict teacher will bring cries of woe and agony.

The Sagittarian has a keen and penetrating mind and usually likes one subject to the exclusion of others. Should the Sagittarian take a fancy to history, then he will become a knowledgeable historian. Should he take a fancy for a special period, say, the Civil War, then he will become an expert! In the lower grades, he will probably take to dinosaurs and be able to rattle off all the names of prehistoric monsters.

Sagittarius likes to move about and dislikes being in one place for too long a time. He tires easily of the same location or situation. He thrives on change. For this reason, never allow the Sagittarian to repeat a year with the same teacher. It will be a complete waste of time and effort.

When John Dewey wrote of learning by doing, he could have been addressing himself to the Sagittarian. Being a sign of action, the Sagittarian child prefers to learn by doing rather than by instruction. Teach him to swim, and he wants to jump right into the water. He has no interest in the preliminaries.

And it can start at a very early age. Only last summer, my

neighbor's four-year-old Sagittarian, who had been watching his father drive the car all his life, decided to take over himself.

One afternoon, when his father left him in the front seat to dash back into the house for a pack of cigarettes, little Eric somehow managed to get behind the wheel, turn on the ignition switch, step on the gas, and take off for town! His father came dashing out of the house, managed to jump into the car and bring it to a halt.

"Eric," said his father, trying not to make it into a traumatic experience, "you know you're not supposed to drive without a license!"

"I have a license!" said Eric, taking his Dad's license out of the dashboard glove compartment.

Chances are "I-Want-To-Right-Now" Sagittarian Eric will be driving often in the next few years unless his father starts locking the car doors.

Open air and sunshine are vital to Sagittarius. He enjoys vigorous outdoor activity and has a natural talent for sports. See to it that your Sagittarian youngster gets lots of outdoor exercise both winter and summer.

Restless by nature, Sagittarius can become nervous and develop nervous habits such as tapping, twirling strands of hair, or nail biting. If you attempt to break a Sagittarian of such a habit, be certain to replace it with something more acceptable. For instance, you might substitute gum chewing for nail biting. Sagittarius children need an outlet for their nervous energy.

One remarkable characteristic of Sagittarians is their complete honesty. Never expect deception or falsehood from this sign. They are so honest that they may appear blunt to the point of rudeness. A Sagittarius sees nothing wrong in calling a spade a spade, even when it might offend someone. He finds it necessary to state unpleasant truths and he may be less than considerate when he does. The Sagittarian child needs intensive instruction in courtesy, kindness, and tact. truthfulness is a splendid trait, but not when it hurts and offends others. The truth can sometimes be a cruel weapon. The overweight playmate of Sagittarius will be told that he is fat, and the poorer student will be told that he is dumb. Expect a few after-school fights over this kind of truthfulness.

A favorite Sagittarian question is "Why?" The Sagittarian can accept almost anything if he is given the reasons for it. More than any other sign of the Zodiac, Sagittarius needs to know the motivations and the causations. In dealing with your Sagittarian child, you will find that explanations are a necessity and can work wonders in getting cooperation.

Sagittarius is optimistic. Those born under this sign are convinced that all will turn out well and that success is just around the corner. They trust in the bounty and goodness of the future. In your school-age Sagittarian, this will manifest itself by an optimism over grades. Even with an "F" on his report card, the Sagittarian truly expects an "A" the next time. This optimism can frustrate a concerned parent and lead one to believe that the child is living in a dream world. No matter how many arguments you present to the contrary, Sagittarius is sure of future success.

One difficulty with the Sagittarian is his love of new projects. He becomes quite excited at the prospect of a new undertaking and will spend hours talking about it and planning it. However, don't expect him to finish it. Sagittarians have a bad habit of giving up before completion. They are full of new ideas and novel projects but their sails lose wind in mid-journey. The Sagittarian child may talk about opening a lemonade stand, may even make the lemonade, but, before long, he is involved with something else. He is stamp-collecting today and building models tomorrow. Because of this trait, he also procrastinates. He will have so much on his mind and be so involved with his latest interest that he may put off the really important business of the moment. His schoolwork may suffer because something else is temporarily more important than homework. The Sagittarian youngster will grow up with less tension and more peace of mind if he can be taught to control his short-lived enthusiasm. Otherwise, his adult life may become bogged down with odds and ends of his own making.

Your Sagittarian child is a freedom-loving, restless, and independent individual. But, he is probably also practical, not lost in the realms of idealism. He is prone to fail to complete what he begins—this is the sign's greatest handicap. Since this sign resents control and authority, and school is only tolerated by the Sagittarian youngster, many Sagittarian children don't take school seriously until they grow older and understand its importance. So, don't give up on your Sagittarian child—chances are you have a "late bloomer" who'll make you a proud parent—eventually.

YOUR SAGITTARIUS CHILD
  (NOVEMBER 23–DECEMBER 21) MAY . . .
get good grades in history and geography
do well in the earth sciences
get only fair grades in mathematics
tend to be slightly sarcastic
be fairly easy to understand
find it hard to deceive you
try to imitate other people's mannerisms
be eager to improve himself
have a wide variety of friends
say "why" and "why not" over and over again
have an insatiable curiosity
be a little careless about his reputation

YOUR SAGITTARIUS CHILD (SCORPIO SIDE,
   NOVEMBER 23–DECEMBER 6) MAY ALSO . . .
be subject to moody highs and lows
be physically strong
show great initiative and overwhelming drive
often be cruel and jealous
show great leadership qualities
have personal magnetism and brilliance
sometimes project an air of mystery
be very ambitious
have great intuition
be able to control his own will

YOUR SAGITTARIUS CHILD (CAPRICORN SIDE,
  DECEMBER 7–DECEMBER 21) MAY ALSO . . .
seem old and wise before his time
be quietly stubborn
have definite tastes and preferences
like order and routine
enjoy family life
tend to have only a few friends
like to do homework
like to dress up or play grown-up
*be a slow learner—but a good scholar after the slow
  start*
be very modest
be totally dependable
seem to be bashful

your child the

capricorn
december 22–january 20
symbol:
the goat
ruling planet: **saturn** • element: **earth**

POSITIVE CHARACTERISTICS:
Reserve, persevering, traditional

NEGATIVE CHARACTERISTICS:
Arrogance, snobbishness, selfishness

GETS ALONG BEST WITH:
Taurus, Virgo, Libra

Little Jack Horner sat in the corner,
Eating a Christmas pie.
He put in his thumb, and pulled out a plum,
And said, "What a good boy am I!"

Modest little Capricorn! Give him a gold star!

The Capricorn youngster is acutely aware of the right thing to do and wants everybody to know that he did it! Overly concerned with the approval of adults, it is almost pathetic to see a Capricorn go to such great lengths to please the teacher or satisfy mother. Capricorn is likely to seem like the classroom goody-goody to the other youngsters or to be viewed with suspicion by brothers and sisters at home. He will never do anything that will harm his reputation and he makes every possible effort to ensure the good opinion of others. It's Capricorn who volunteers to do the dishes or wash the chalkboards. It's Capricorn who upholds everything that parents or teacher says.

If your local school gives a good citizenship award, I'll wager that the winner is a Capricorn. But, sometimes, those admirable character traits can deteriorate into plain old-fashioned snitching.

I remember sitting in the faculty dining room with a group of teachers and listening to them talk about what a good boy Charles is.

"Yes, that's true," said his current teacher, "but he is driving me crazy with all his petty snitching. He's always telling me who passed a note and little things that I'd just as soon not know about." The teacher was more concerned over Charles' unpopularity with the other children than about the slight infractions he reports.

"Next time he snitches about some minor infraction," I suggested, "send him on to me without making it seem like punishment."

I went back to my office and checked the records to make certain what I already suspected: Charles is a Capricorn. And that very afternoon, the teacher sent him on to me after he'd reported somebody for whispering during study period.

At that time, I was inaugurating a new safety patrol system in the school and Charles seemed like an excellent choice. I explained to him that as Safety Patrolman he would be required to see that all the regulations were followed.

"But, remember, Charles," I explained, "don't be so involved in minor harmless infractions that you miss the bigger, more dangerous ones."

Charles got the message and over the next few weeks managed to learn to differentiate between picayune snitching and reporting major infractions.

So, you see, some annoying Capricorn habits can be converted into definite assets to the child and the community.

Capricorn children accept school in good spirit and are usually exemplary students, especially in conduct and citizenship. The Capricorn is steady and dependable in his efforts to succeed, and parents will seldom have to urge Capricorns to do homework or tend to their chores.

This sign likes everything to be on a firm and solid foundation. It is very exacting and sometimes very demanding. The Capricorn child is not always easy to please. He wants his toys to work and his clothing to fit, and he can become very unhappy over seemingly insignificant imperfections.

Although the Capricorn youngster tends toward scrappiness with other children, he is somewhat strained in his overall relationship with his peers. He likes to argue, but never for argument's sake, and he will rarely start a quarrel, but once in it, he will see it through to the bitter end. The Capricorn sometimes conveys an attitude of "knock the chip off my shoulder," and, as a result, finds himself embroiled in hostile situations. The Capricorn child needs help in overcoming this attitude and in learning to project a more positive personality.

The Capricorn, like Scorpio, is a long-lived sign. Most Capricorns are rugged and healthy although they like to dwell on sickness and death. Your Capricorn child may be prone to hypochondria, as a result. They seem to enjoy illness and take pleasure in a recitation of symptoms. It would be wise to underplay illness or physical discomfort around the Capricorn youngster or it may trigger his sympathetic interest.

Capricorn's nature is basically utilitarian and he tends to be reluctant to dispose of anything. Your Capricorn boy or girl may have a cluttered bedroom—dresser drawers may resemble a squirrel's nest. They love to gather and save and tend to their possessions. This tendency also applies to their friends. Long after a friendship is dissolved, the Capricorn child will continue to discuss it. He can never completely discard anything—even people!

Position and recognition are extremely important to Capricorn. It is an ambitious sign and knows how to attain success. The Capricorn is effective in the employment of tact, diplomacy, and self-expression. He will not flout convention or tradition and is inclined to be overly conservative. His natural instinct is to do nothing openly to which others might object. Interestingly enough, in his secret life, he may be the exact opposite of what he represents. To Capricorn, it's not the deed as much as others' reactions to the deed.

Your Capricorn child tends to imitate those he admires. Don't be too surprised should he begin talking like the teacher or behaving like a favorite relative. This imitation is, once again, Capricorn's way of aiming to please.

As a student, Capricorn is a plodder. He has persistence and will make every effort to overcome obstacles. Sometimes this stamina is close to amazing. The Capricorn works hard for all he gets. Although he has a good mind, he has some difficulty in expressing himself. He tends to shy away from answering in class and would rather die than recite in front of the class. As long as he can study quietly at his desk and not talk, he will do well. If pushed into group discussions or forced to recite, Capricorn may rebel and develop a negative attitude toward school and teacher.

Capricorn needs security. He needs the feeling of belonging and of future stability. For this reason, the Capricorn child is a joiner. Boy Scouts, Girl Scouts, Little League, and church groups will attract him. These groups satisfy the need for peer approval and social acceptance. He likes to belong and to have a sense of identity, and he will be an active member of his group. Many Capricorns tend to remain in their groups until adulthood. The Capricorn Boy Scout grows into the Capricorn Man Scout.

Capricorn is a kind and thoughtful sign. The Capricorn child will never rest until a favor is returned or a kindness is reciprocated. You need never worry about your Capricorn in this regard. He is naturally courteous and considerate. There will be times when you will be astonished at his consideration and thoughtfulness.

An amusing aspect of this characteristic is Capricorn's method of gift-giving and gift selection. Capricorn uses himself and his own interests in deciding on gifts. Consequently, many of Capricorn's gifts are puzzling and one may get the impression that the gift really didn't get much thought. Don't be shocked when you get a baseball glove for Mother's Day or a doll for Father's Day. This is just Capricorn's way! He's convinced that what pleases him is sure to please you, and he feels that he is paying you a great compliment.

Capricorn children may demonstrate an early interest in boy-girl relationships. They have a pronounced consciousness of sex difference and can be quite flirtatious. Romantic attachments are of great interest to this sign and they are only too pleased to announce the names of their current boyfriends or girlfriends. In adolescence, this interest is amplified.

Sometimes the interest in sex is amplified a bit too much and gets distorted. At a recent PTA meeting, one of the mothers mentioned to me that her daughter, Pia, told her that two of our teachers were involved in a serious romance.

I investigated quietly and found that it just wasn't true. I also found that Pia was a Capricorn and thus overly interested in affairs of romance.

I talked it over with the teacher who was the adviser of the school newspaper and, together, we agreed that Pia would make an excellent society columnist. It was a way to make constructive use of her sun sign characteristic.

Pia loved the idea and accepted the position with great enthusiasm.

However, the first column she submitted led off with the following item: "What pretty French teacher is seeing what handsome Math teacher after class every day?"

In summary, your Capricorn child may be outstanding in his conscientious ways and his determination to please others. Very aware of tradition and law, he will probably refrain from doing anything that might jeopardize his social position or his reputation. He is a hard worker and his efforts usually pay dividends.

Your Capricorn child is the solid citizen of the younger set!

Your Capricorn Child
(December 22–January 20) May . . .
do well in the social sciences
get good grades in scientific subjects
get only fair grades in foreign languages
be very practical
be very conscious of dress and deportment
be slightly snobbish
greatly admire the success of others
tend to meddle in the affairs of others
like to observe anniversaries and holidays

YOUR CAPRICORN CHILD (SAGITTARIUS SIDE,
DECEMBER 22–JANUARY 5) MAY ALSO . . .

be friendly and relaxed
have good hunches
be very straightforward
always seem optimistic
win with a smile
resent being contained
object to bias and discrimination
run away because of his urge to travel
make difficult jobs seem easy
combine luck with good judgment
be successful at almost everything he tries
be not so much an innovator as a doer

YOUR CAPRICORN CHILD (AQUARIUS SIDE,
  JANUARY 6–JANUARY 20) MAY ALSO . . .
be sensitive and stubborn
be inventive and original
constantly get involved in new projects
adopt an anything-goes kind of personality
reveal very contradictory traits
have unexpected reactions to things
sometimes be a late starter
use instinct rather than logic
be considered eccentric by others
go his own way
develop many friendly relationships

your child the

aquarius
january 21–february 19
symbol:

the water-bearer
ruling planet: **uranus** • element: **air**

POSITIVE CHARACTERISTICS:
  Humaneness, honesty, sociability

NEGATIVE CHARACTERISTICS:
  Rebellion, impatience, absentmindedness

GETS ALONG BEST WITH:
  Libra, Gemini, Aries

> *O do you know the muffin man,*
> *The muffin man, the muffin man?*

Are you kidding? Aquarius knows everybody!

The typical Aquarian is not happy unless he is with others. This is an exceedingly social sign. Consequently, the Aquarian youngster likes school because he enjoys the social contact of a group situation. He may be a trifle reluctant about returning to school after a summer of fun, because he has had too many good times doing things that interested him. He may consider school "dull" at first but it will soon permeate his thinking and be accepted.

This Aquarian trait of extreme sociability can often be utilized productively in human relationships. The married teenage daughter of a cousin of mine recently used her Aquarian sun sign to good advantage.

Linda married a delightful young man who was fortunate enough to have a responsible position in business. Her husband recognized that her Aquarian traits made her sensitive to the feelings of others, and he confided in her the office personnel problems and his personal relationships with his bosses. Like a true Aquarian, she took great exception to any associates who criticized her husband, but understood the motivation as well.

It began to become apparent to Linda that things were not going too well for her husband. Conflicts had arisen between him and the company's top executive. Linda listened to her husband's version of the disagreement, then took the situation into her own hands. She called the boss's wife and invited them to dinner.

During that pleasant evening, Linda's charm and diplomacy managed to bring the conflict into the open in an indirect way and within an hour all major points of friction were resolved.

Thus, Linda's Aquarian charm and sociability paid dividends for her husband who soon after got a promotion.

However, knowing the sometimes over-friendly ways of a

true Aquarian, I'd keep my eye on that boss and my wife, if I were the husband.

The Aquarian student may seem slow in everything but the subject that interests him. Aquarians are prone to like or dislike with intensity. You rarely meet an Aquarian with a neutral position. They are outspoken and love to give their opinion, even when not asked! Never ask an Aquarian for advice unless you want it and then be prepared for a straight and sometimes harsh answer! His instinct is good as is his desire to help, but his sincerity is too sharp for comfort. Your Aquarian child will tell you just what she thinks of her dinner or the new dress you bought her. If it doesn't please Aquarius, you'll know it, and it won't be couched in diplomatic terms.

Aquarians have a dogged determination and inventive minds. They have an enviable fixity of purpose and they are not satisfied until they finish what they start. Notice this in your Aquarian child—he will always finish building his model or coloring his picture book.

Once an Aquarian makes up his mind, it is made up! He has difficulty altering his position or changing his opinion. Thankfully, the Aquarian usually recognizes this individual difficulty although he may do little to control it. The Aquarian youngster will "absolutely adore" a teacher or "absolutely hate" another. For the former, little Aquarius will work overtime to please. For the latter, little Aquarius will do nothing. The teacher-pupil relationship is extremely important in the Aquarian school life.

Aquarians have a natural gift for concentration and precision. Watch your Aquarian child read—he will pronounce every word with determination. The Aquarian youngster is not a good candidate for speed reading! In every task that the Aquarian undertakes, this passion for precision is very obvious. In doing an arithmetic problem, the Aquarian youngster follows every step and is horrified when you suggest a shortcut. Aquarians are not always the easiest children to help with their homework.

The Aquarian is a humanitarian and is very much concerned with the larger social problems. It is said that the Aquarian can see a starving neighbor and yet be more concerned with starvation in India. His views tend to be global rather than local. He takes on the burdens of mankind and really wants to do something about them. Your Aquarian child will reveal this idealistic tendency early in life and may astound you with his intuitive understanding of social and international problems. Obviously, history will hold a certain fascination for him as he grows more aware of the world. The Aquarian is also a great newspaper reader. You will notice your Aquarian child reading the newspaper with an interest usually reserved for an adult.

Aquarius is attracted by the new and the fashionable. Your Aquarian youngster will want the latest fashion in clothing and will be very aware of what is in and what is out. Never attempt to tame this interest as it will be an almost impossible task. It will be easier and more comfortable for all concerned if you allow your Aquarian to be in style and learn to live with the fads and fashions. The Aquarian youngster often thinks his parents are old-fashioned anyway!

This sign likes the feeling of having worked for what he has attained. As a rule, the Aquarian does not do things in a daring or irresponsible way and will never work the angles in order to succeed. He wants only those benefits that come to him as a result of effort expended. He works and he gets results. Your Aquarian child may frustrate you at times with this attitude. For example, if he thinks his report card or test grade is too high and is not representative of his effort, he will feel compelled to ask the teacher for a lower grade. He wants his due, but not more than that.

The Aquarian loves people and loves being with people. He has a good personality and is likely to bubble with good spirits. Aquarians smile and do it easily. Yet, despite this good nature, they lack patience with others. When the Aquarian has lost his temper, it is usually because he has lost his patience. The Aquarians have a low boiling point when it comes to tolerance and forebearance. Often it seems that the Aquarian will excuse in himself what he will not excuse in others.

To others, the Aquarian seems lucky. Good things seem to happen to him and everything always seems to work out to his advantage. From an astrological point of view, this is explained by the cyclic period which is currently favorable to the sign of Aquarius. This period will continue for many years and all Aquarians will benefit and reap their harvest of good fortune.

This sign is known for its loyalty to friends and loved ones. Your Aquarian child will probably always be a dutiful son or daughter and will pay you respect and deference all through your life. Aquarians make good friends and good sons and daughters. Their loyalty is never short-lived.

In summary, the Aquarian child is utilitarian and inventive. He has determination and enjoys the fruits of his labor. He has strong likes and dislikes and can be highly opinionated. He enjoys giving advice and wants to help others. He is a friendly person and radiates warmth and social concern. The sign of Aquarius is philosophical and interested in the larger problems of living. He is loyal and can be a trusted friend.

All told, your Aquarian youngster has been greatly blessed by the heavens—and so have you!

YOUR AQUARIAN CHILD
  (JANUARY 21–FEBRUARY 19) MAY . . .
get good grades in the social sciences
get only fair grades in mathematics
have success in mastering another language
show a native shrewdness
be a good judge of character
smile easily but seldom laugh
make friends easily but have some difficulty in maintaining a steady friendship
frequently have his "foot in his mouth"
spend too much time with trifles
worry about the state of the world—and try to do something about it!

Your Aquarian Child (Capricorn Side,
    January 21–February 4) May Also . . .
refuse to take no for an answer
be willing to work hard to gain victory
not very often be amused
sometimes be a bit of a loner
appear selfish because of honest ambition
need positions of power
hate to make mistakes
be practical about money
help out when the problems crop up

Your Aquarian Child (Pisces Side,
    February 5–February 19) May Also . . .
be a born charmer
tend to daydream
be a bit psychic
hate to abide by rules and schedules
get his own way in a subtle fashion
need constant reminders of how good he is
often seem to be off in a world of his own
be agile on his feet
like abstract things
have moments of slight irresponsibility
be sensitive and tearful at times
find it hard to tell lies from imagination
need to be pushed—but not too hard

your child the

pisces
february 20–march 20
symbol:
the fishes
ruling planet: **neptune and jupiter** •
element: **water**

POSITIVE CHARACTERISTICS:
Reverence, compassion, sensitivity
NEGATIVE CHARACTERISTICS:
Melancholia, dreaminess, egocentricity
GETS ALONG BEST WITH:
Cancer, Scorpio, Virgo
Pease-porridge hot,
Pease-porridge cold,
Pease-porridge in the pot,
Nine days old.

But don't expect your Pisces child to eat it!
Chances are he's a picky eater and will have to be
coaxed to try anything which his good judgment tells
him is likely to be rancid. Nine days old!

On the whole, though, Pisces is a receptive sign and the chances are your Pisces child has a natural ability for sizing up a person or a situation. This can be a definite asset in the classroom. Pisces knows instinctively what a teacher wants and he knows how to please the teacher. However, until Pisces is sure of himself, he will cling to past security.

You will notice the Piscean child clutching mother on that first day of school. Yet, once he is sure of his ground, he lets go and becomes independent. This sometimes manifests itself after summer vacation. For the first few weeks of school, the Piscean child may malinger or want to stay home. This is only a temporary reaction to a new situation. It will pass.

Pisces is such a receptive sign that there are certain dangers to beware of. Pisces tends to fall in easily with the ideas and activities of each person he is with. He is so in tune with other people that he may take on their ways and he must be helped in overcoming this somewhat dangerous affinity. Parents must be on guard to protect their Pisces youngster from bad companions and unhealthy situations. Pisces can be easily persuaded and easily led astray. With this sign, it is of prime importance that you know where the child is and with whom.

Due to the native receptivity of the sign, the Piscean child will do well in school. He learns easily and seems to absorb knowledge like a sponge soaks up liquid. He can please the teacher with little effort and he has an excellent memory. The Piscean memory should be utilized. Pisces can commit things to memory with little effort and it would be a shame to waste this talent.

The Piscean child will more than likely show an interest in religion and the more serious side of living. Sunday School and church will fascinate him, although Pisces may ask embarrassingly curious questions there. Pisces can be a true believer and scrupulously religious.

All aspects of the occult may also fascinate your Pisces child—everything from goblins to séances. Magic, too.

Ninth-grader Piscean Jim was a cause of much worry to his family because he was so involved in mysticism. When he started making all his decisions on the basis of the *I Ching*, his father asked me if I thought he needed psychological help.

After consulting with a therapist, I decided to try to direct Jim's Piscean interest in the occult into other channels.

Sleight-of-hand magic, I reasoned, is really an art form— and, for some reason, more acceptable to society as an active pastime.

I told Jim that his parents had told me of his interest in the mystic and suggested that he might want to try his hand with a magic act during the next school assembly. He accepted the offer enthusiastically. According to his father, Jim practiced day and night for the whole week. The act was an enormous success at the assembly.

Soon, Jim was earning money performing at children's parties and church socials. It was a perfect example of how a Piscean interest in psychic phenomena and mysticism can be channeled into profitable enterprises.

Yes, our society looks askance at séances—but it looks less askance if there's a charge of $5 a head.

The Piscean child usually has a vivid and active imagination. You will begin to notice this while your Pisces is very young. He will make up fantastic stories and his playthings take on very real personalities. The teddy bear and the doll become persons and have fictitious lives of their own. Frequently, the Piscean child creates an imaginary playmate of an animal friend and will speak of it so convincingly that the parent is made to wonder. One Pisces girl I know invented a sheep dog and kept it alive in her imagination until her mid-teens.

Pisces is a born artist with a keen sense of color and form.

The Piscean child loves to color and will probably ask for a set of crayons or watercolors with all the various hues and tones. He won't settle for a simple eight-color set! Pisces is experimental in his art work and some of his childhood drawings may indicate great talent. He is often not terribly realistic in his representations. His sky may be orange and his landscape purple. If asked to explain his choices, the answer "it's pretty" probably satisfies him.

Pisces may also demonstrate dramatic ability and love to mimic and impersonate. He can take on the aura of his environment and re-create a situation or experience. You will probably enjoy his stories and tales from school. He can often imitate people with clarity and realism and many an unsuspecting teacher is cleverly mimicked at home. In this same vein, Pisces likes to imitate the mannerisms of his favorite people. Your Pisces child may adopt his teacher's colloquialisms or a favorite uncle's behavior patterns. From time to time, you may wonder where he has picked something up. Look to his friends and family for your clue.

It is most unfortunate that many Pisceans tend to procrastinate and try to avoid unpleasant situations. Pisces will wait until the last moment of pain before going to the dentist, and even then, may procrastinate further! It would be wise to help your Pisces child overcome this potentially dangerous trait. Notice how long he can tolerate an unpleasant situation before he acts. Imagine the implications in his adult life!

Pisces is a naturally happy and successful person but he may have a negative side. Because of his extreme sensitivity, Pisces can lunge out at others who annoy him. Expect an occasional tantrum from your Piscean youngster but remember that it is only his way of masking his own uncertainty and sensitivity. When Pisces is perfectly attuned, he is in full command of himself and the situation.

Pisces has a strong sense of exactness and precision and can be very happy doing detailed work. However, as soon as detail becomes routine, then it becomes drudgery for the Piscean. An arithmetic problem will be carefully executed but an assignment of five or ten problems every night will bring complaints and protests.

The personality of Pisces is full of schemes and dreams. It can dream up elaborate plans but rarely put them into motion. Pisces talks but does not act. The danger here is that Pisces might neglect important work and responsibilities to dwell on some new idea. Help your Piscean child to conquer this tendency, especially with school assignments. Force him to stick with the task at hand and save his dreaming for an idle moment. And don't be too surprised when the school complains of daydreaming in class.

On the whole, your Pisces child is a pleasant and happy sign. It is a supersensitive one and can "tune in" on people and events. Used to advantage, this gift can bring fame and fortune. Misused, it can bring trouble. Pisces is artistic and dramatic and loves color and form. It is a religious and supernatural sign and concerns itself with thoughts of piety and morality.

A warning: In this age of drug abuse, be watchful of your Piscean child. Some astrologers claim that this sign is especially prone to the use of drugs and barbiturates!

Your Pisces Child
  (February 20–March 20) May . . .
have some artistic ability
get good grades in the artistic subjects
get only fair grades in history, geography, and health
have a retiring disposition
be somewhat excitable
be occasionally morose
have a pallid complexion
be an anxiety to you
like the sea
have bursts of temper
enjoy drama

YOUR PISCES CHILD (AQUARIAN SIDE,
  FEBRUARY 20–MARCH 5) MAY ALSO . . .
show great individuality
accept everybody
be an original thinker . . . often with great depth
have a memory like an elephant
reveal an insatiable curiosity
be at home anywhere with anybody doing anything
have very high ideals
tend to put things off
hate routine details
prove to be a rebel—usually with a cause
be self-consciously different sometimes
be honest and warm

Your Pisces Child (Aries Side,
   March 6–March 20) May Also . . .
like to be the boss
be difficult eater
tend to be accident prone
be very curious—even a bit of a peeping tom
be openly affectionate
reveal short, explosive fury, quickly replaced by an-
   gelic generosity
hate to do homework
react well to real challenge
combine wild imagination with practicality
be impatient
tend to be a bit of a bully
need to be praised constantly
start and stop innumerable projects
have a constantly changing set of idols

7

Disciplining and Motivating the Sun Signs

I walked into the school cafeteria the other day and noticed a fifth-grade black girl engrossed in a booklet while she munched on her sandwich and milk. Curious, I edged close enough to read the title of the book—it was *Arlene Dahl's Beautyscope For Geminis.*

"Brenda," I asked, "what have you learned about yourself from that book?"

She looked at me and sighed.

"Dr. Loeper," she said, "it's purple eye shadow for me—all the way!"

Now, I hope that the readers of this book will get just a bit more out of astrology than that little girl did. As parents, probably the most important thing you may obtain is help in disciplining and motivating your child, based in part upon your knowledge of his sun sign, and yours.

I have attempted here to suggest some disciplinary techniques appropriate to the various sun signs. But this is not the whole story. Discipline is more than what you do *after* things have gone wrong. It is also something you do to ensure that things go right. Discipline is a harsh word when it is associated with punishment alone, but it can be a comforting word when it is viewed as a total procedure.

This is where so many parents go wrong. They see discipline only as punitive medicine and not as preventive. It is really the total training that a child receives from infancy to teens. And there are certain things that work with all children, and certain needs that are true of all the sun signs.

All children need love and affection. It is of tremendous importance and without it there is little security or confidence. A parent is not a dictator who issues rules and regulations, but a person who comforts and understands. Before children will obey, they must trust and this trust will be built up over the years. It will come out of being consistent in your relationships, fair in your decisions, and warm in your affection.

All children need a sense of self-respect. They must think well of themselves if they are to think well of others. They must feel that they have rights as individuals and have some share in making selections and decisions in the planning of their own lives. Parents must avoid making all the decisions, and allow children to explore and learn by doing. Situations should be created that will give young people responsibility and choices. When children are free to express feelings, concerns, and interests, they will grow in self-respect.

All children need freedom from fear. Fears create tensions and only intensify an unpleasant situation. Don't try to scare children and don't try to intimidate them. Extreme approaches will bring on extreme reactions. Rather try to handle your child in a calm, gentle, firm manner. Be a realist and not a perfectionist. Let your child know that for every act there is a consequence, and always be satisfied with improvement.

Finally, all children need praise and a sense of accomplishment. Make certain that you praise your child as often as you criticize him. Recognize his achievements and reward his good efforts. If you are positive and complimentary to your child when he does what is expected of him, you will spend less time correcting him.

The sun signs identify a personality and indicate effective moods of discipline, but this is only part of the picture. There are other parts and they cannot be ignored.

Motivation is the incentive that causes people to act. It can be external influence or it can be an interior impulse. Some people respond to an enticement or an allurement. They are motivated by prizes or rewards. Others are self-motivated and do things because of an inner desire to act in one way or another.

In this section, I also offer suggestions for motivating the sun signs. Some are easier to motivate than others. Some are more self-motivated while others need outside encouragement. But, in motivating anyone, it is important to be realistic.

One can only do what is within capabilities. No matter how hard you tried or how cleverly you devised it, you could never motivate a baby to lift a three-hundred-pound weight. Motivation is the spur that turns a potentiality into a reality. It brings about the possible. It cannot bring about the impossible.

The sun signs offer clues to proper motivation but they are limited by the facts of reality. They offer help only with reasonable demands and sensible expectations.

ARIES

Joan loves to win. She's a fourth grader in school . . . and a typical Arien youngster with a lively personality and native humor. Talented in art, the only time she'll employ her gift is when there's a contest to be won.

At the beginning of last year, Joan worked overtime to produce a winning safety poster. But, once the prize was hers, to my dismay Joan's interest in art projects completely dissipated.

"Art classes are dumb!" was Joan's comment. She feels that further lessons are "A waste of time."

Although Joan is intellectually gifted, she is an underachiever in school. Both her teachers and her parents feel that she could do better. However, her main interest in school is not the classroom instruction but her little circle of classroom friends. She is the leader of this group and will challenge anyone who tries to usurp her position. It is usually Joan who decides what games the group will play or what new student will be admitted to her inner circle. She is very much in charge of things, to the point of being considered pushy by some of her girlfriends.

Joan has a great sense of fun and can be a little on the wild side. Her frivolity must be curbed or she can get carried away. The other children enjoy being with her and like the sense of excitement she can generate. In typical Arien fashion, Joan hero-worships a sixth-grade boy named Peter. She will tolerate no criticism of Peter from the other children. Critical herself—but nobody else.

Joan is always dashing off on some new venture. She is making doll clothes today and learning to bicycle tomorrow. She seems to crave novelty and change and is happiest when there is something new to anticipate. Her teachers comment on this trait frequently.

Right now, Joan is taking swimming lessons—there are prizes to be won and she is determined to win them. But her parents and I realize that as soon as the blue ribbon is captured, she won't go near the pool; in fact, she will look upon swimming with contempt.

I have conferred with her mother and father and they are worried that Joan will follow the same pattern throughout her life. Her mother, in particular, is worried about Joan's future marital status.

"After she's won the big prize—a husband—will she find enough challenge in marriage?" she asked.

There's no question about it, Joan's Arien qualities may very well create a problem for her. Perhaps in school we will be able to offer her regular prizes for achievement at the end of each stage of her learning. Eventually, she may thus acquire the urge to learn for learning's sake.

But the current knowledge of her tendencies through studying her sun sign is actually a great help to us—Joan's teachers and parents—in training her to cope now with character traits which could prove troublesome later on!

Disciplining and Motivating Aries

Aries is an intellectual sign, characterized by braininess. Children of this sign are full of confidence and optimism, and rarely hampered by shyness or pessimism. They can project pleasure into the future despite any present difficulties. As a result of these qualities, many guidance measures will prove totally ineffective with this sign.

Spank an Aries today, and it will be forgotten tomorrow. Scold an Aries today, and it will be past history tomorrow. Ariens don't seem to learn by experience; you may notice that your Arien child will display little carry-over, and that you must correct the same errors over and over again.

The best and most effective way of guiding an Arien child is to deny him some anticipated pleasure. Because of their optimism and forward-looking attitude, Ariens are more concerned about limits in the future rather than in the present. Rather than an immediate measure, try denying anticipated pleasure—television, dessert, allowance, or weekend privileges. This will usually motivate an Arien to cooperate.

Gregory is a good example of the way an Arien child reacts. For quite a while his mother has been trying to get him to straighten out his room and put away the clothing that lies on the floor, on chairs, anywhere, if she doesn't constantly pick up after him. Her habit has been to lecture him each time, and she wonders why he doesn't respond.

The answer is simply that she's attacking the problem in the present, which handling he abides and forgets. Actually, she would get much quicker results if she were to limit his future pleasures in the ways I have described. Gregory is a bright, buoyant child, ever so much more concerned with tomorrow than he is with today.

It is important to note that a parent should never waste time lecturing an Arien child or explaining the impropriety of his poor behavior. He may understand what you are saying, but he won't really listen. Aries can concentrate on the present but the present is an ever-changing thing. What is true today may not be true tomorrow—and your Arien child knows that.

Aries children are most easily motivated with rewards. As a parent, make certain that those rewards are spiritual as well as monetary.

To allow an Arien child to develop a pattern of working for material rewards alone will limit his enjoyment of a rich and satisfying adulthood. So use this technique wisely and with prudence.

As he grows, try substituting more distant and more abstract rewards for the immediate and concrete ones. Luring a sixth-grade Arien with dollars is one thing, but it could be tragic if it developed into a pattern in senior high school. The high-school-age Arien should be working for the distant rewards of a secure future and a good job. Ensuring this is your responsibility as a parent.

Another Arien motivation is the desire for superiority. Aries likes to excell and to be among the best. If your Arien child has been blessed with a special talent, encourage him to capitalize on it. An Arien pianist or an Arien artist can reach the peaks of perfection if properly motivated. He wants to be the best and you can help him with encouragement and praise. Keep in mind that Aries likes himself but he wants you to like him as well. His self-image is good and positive but it needs polishing and reassurance from those he loves. Always encourage an Arien with praise and approbation. It will pay dividends in increased effort and renewed dedication.

TAURUS

"Here's my report on our vacation in San Juan," Billy said shyly as he handed in his latest contribution to the school newspaper.

I withheld any outward signs of despair but I already knew what to expect—a poorly written story filled with great amounts of dull detail.

Billy is a hard worker and is considered an overachiever by most of his teachers. But, even when he lacks ability—as in journalism—he will try to put forth great effort. Last year he volunteered for the school paper, despite his difficulties with English. Although almost all of his contributions are badly done, Billy hands in articles regularly. He doesn't seem to recognize that his writing is really less than adequate.

Billy's birthday is April 30, right in the middle of the Taurus span. And this determination of his is a predictable characteristic.

Like many Taurus children, Billy is husky, enjoys eating, is a constant nibbler. His every move is made with a conscious deliberation.

Billy is a pleasant child and well-liked by the other children. He has a few close friends and they are inseparable. They play together to the exclusion of other children. When Billy's father tried to expand his son's circle of friends by having him join Indian Guides, the plan backfired. Billy talked his friends into joining along with him. His loyalty to these boys is constant and there is much concern every year about classroom assignments. Billy has even suggested to the teacher that he be placed with his friends.

For Billy, the anticipation is always greater than the realization. Christmas is anxiously awaited and talked about, yet Christmas morning seems anticlimactic. Last year, Billy was so excited during December that his parents thought Christmas Day would be great fun. Yet, on Christmas, Billy was almost glum; his parents couldn't understand why he didn't seem too interested in his new toys.

Eventually I found that Billy's enormous drive and determination made him a likely prospect for selling the newspaper to the other students. And as soon as I made him circulation manager, he happily concentrated all his efforts in that area.

It was a relief not to have to read those contributions!

Disciplining and Motivating Taurus

Typical of his sun sign, the Taurus child is steadfast and persistent. Even when faced with difficulties, Taurus will manifest an amazing determination and frequently show little fear. He cannot be easily frightened or intimidated.

Obviously, these strong characteristics have certain implications when the time comes to discipline a Taurus youngster. Being strong-willed and stubborn, a Taurus child is very difficult to handle when these attributes are forced to the surface. In a situation requiring some disciplinary action, you can be certain that Taurus will employ all his defenses and make your job twice as difficult.

Firmness is essential and the Taurus child will usually respect a firm approach. You must always show strength in dealing with Taurus and never allow a trace of weakness or sympathy to seep into your confrontation. You can't mix emotions with Taurus. Don't try to be stern and loving at the same time and forget about the "it will hurt me more than it will hurt you" routine. Taurus will interpret this as a sign of weakness and a crack in your fortifications. You are dealing with a stubborn sign and you must meet force with force.

You can also expect a display of emotions. There may be tears, wailing, even kicking. The neighbors may be ready to call the police and accuse you of child-beating. But despite this, remain strong. This is merely Taurus fighting back and when Taurus fights, every weapon is used to advantage. Taurus children can really put on a good show! Bill is a Taurus and he can work himself into a frenzy. When you look at his tear-stained face, you are tempted to relent. And this is exactly what that tear-stained face wants you to do!

Neither physical punishment nor denial has much effect on Taurus. He just doesn't care if you spank him, and taking away television will be a waste of time. When discipline is necessary, demand Taurus's cooperation with strong words and a stern tone. If he senses that you mean it, he will abdicate his position and meet your demands. On the other hand, if he senses any weakness or indecision, you've lost the battle. With Taurus, a show of strength, even if it is only a good bluff, is your best method of discipline.

Another warning to parents of Taurus. Don't nag. If Taurus children are nagged sufficiently, their wrath will be aroused and you will be sorry that you did it. Nagging wears them down and they will strike back with vehemence. They

141

can be very obedient if handled correctly. They must know what is expected of them and they want consistency. They associate nagging with weakness, inconsistency and malice. The surest way to lose touch with your Taurus child is to pick away at him with petty concerns and complaints.

Because it is an earth sign, Taurus loves material comfort. Taurus children can be motivated by offering some reward for good behavior. They will respond to this technique but not as a steady procedure, which Taurus might interpret as parental deficiency and take advantage of. Use rewards sparingly.

The ease with which you can motivate Taurus children depends on the intensity of the Taurus traits in the individual child. Usually Taurus will respond to structure and discipline, wants to cooperate, and can be motivated by a plea for cooperation.

However, a Taurus child who is excessively stubborn or grossly materialistic may be difficult to motivate. In a case like this, it is best to take advantage of another Taurus characteristic. Taurus children are not aggressive and are prone to avoid any direct confrontation. If they know that you are just as determined to have them do something as they are not to do it, they will relent. Don't goad them and don't push them into a corner. Just show determination and strength.

Always remember that the symbol of Taurus is the bull. In a bullfight, the matador must convince the bull of his superiority and cleverness. He does this through bravery and manipulation. A bullfight is not as much a physical struggle as it is a battle of wits and nerves. The same approach is true of any conflict with your Taurus child. You cannot weaken and you can never be off your guard. The fury of an aroused Taurus can be an awful thing. On the other hand, the cooperation and good humor of a properly handled Taurus can be a joy and a comfort.

GEMINI

Tommy was always in trouble in my class for not completing his assignments. This bright 10-year-old was getting bad grades—and I knew he really had the capability of doing much better work.

So, I checked his sun sign—sure enough, young Tommy was a Gemini. But his May 23 birthday put him on the Taurus cusp. Not only did he have the Gemini characteristic of difficulty in keeping interest in such prosaic things as homework, but he was exhibiting the Taurus characteristic of finding it hard to accept any sort of criticism.

I conferred with Tommy's parents and they explained that Aunt Mildred and Uncle Harry have "spoiled" Tommy. Anything he asks for is their command. They have loaded him down with toys and gifts and Tommy seems to enjoy their attention. He tends to play these relatives against his parents. When his parents refuse a request, Tommy runs to Aunt and Uncle.

Tommy always has a new best friend. Each new child he meets becomes his best friend for the next few days. The house is always filled with new faces because Tommy is always making new friends. He forgets them as quickly as he makes them.

An interesting Gemini trait in Tommy is his love of short-cuts. He is always telling you about a new short-cut to school, a new short-cut to church or a new short-cut he has devised in sweeping the yard. Despite his short-cuts, it takes him longer than usual to get anywhere or do anything.

Tommy is always late. When he goes out to play before dinner, his mother never quite knows when he will return or where he has been. When he finally does show up, he always has a convenient excuse. Despite scolding and punishment,

Tommy is still late. He is usually the child seen running to catch the school bus in the morning. One day, the driver had to wait over five minutes while Tommy ran back home to get his books.

Well, what were we to do about the immediate problem—Tommy's consistent inability to do his homework? I told his father that they were going to have to put Tommy on a rigid schedule and send him to his room every evening to do his homework. And they would have to make constant room checks—for the chances are that Tommy would be doodling, playing with his pencils, or reading something completely removed from the school work at hand.

Tommy's parents tried this; little by little, they were able to establish a new homework pattern for Tommy. But, it wasn't an easy job, and it wasn't a quick one because at every opportunity Tommy would try to slip back into the old pattern of procrastination.

After all, Tommy was acting according to his sun sign pattern and it is never easy to break such a pattern.

Disciplining and Motivating Gemini

Gemini is an exuberant sign that loves change. It is stimulated by newness and exploration. It is a social sign that reaches out to other people and wants to be involved. It is always seeking novelty and diversification. Variety is the essence of the Gemini spirit.

Using this as a premise, it is obvious that confinement and restriction can be difficult punishments for a Gemini child. When there is a need for some disciplinary action, you might send Gemini to his room for a few hours or tell him not to leave the house. Any limitation on his action will bring quick results. Geminis don't like to be held down or confined, and this, to their way of thinking, is the worst sentence you could pass. They can withstand spankings and scoldings but they dread isolation.

Tracy is a Gemini child, and her parents have discovered that simply asking her to stand in the corner for a short period works wonders. This is an old-fashioned way of handling a child, but perhaps it was originally devised for the gentle discipline that Gemini children respond to. It works with Tracy and it will probably work with other children of this sign. To separate Gemini from the excitement of his world and from the zest of everyday living is highly effective in assuring his cooperation.

Keep in mind that as a general rule it is wise to allow your Gemini child to follow his own erratic course. It may confuse you and you may not understand, but do not attempt to superimpose your ways on his. If you realize the Gemini love of variety, you can avert many discipline problems. Do not expect consistency from your Gemini youngster and do not chide him for inconsistency. This is a manifestation of his restless nature. Remember that the sign of Gemini is the twin. Gemini is one today and another tomorrow. When you discipline Gemini, be certain that you are attacking the issue at hand and not the pattern.

To punish a Gemini child for inconsistent behavior would be foolish. This is the way he is. To punish him for a precise and clearly defined misdeed is another thing entirely.

A parent has an advantage with this sign. Isolation and confinement are relatively easy measures to enforce. You don't need to waste too many words on a Gemini.

In either disciplining or motivating a Gemini child, another method can be employed to advantage. Gemini loves sympathy. He wants others, especially those close to him, to feel his disappointments and understand his frustrations. When he fails, he wants you to understand his bitter disappointment with himself over his failure. A clever use of sympathy can manipulate a Gemini child. Gemini responds to sympathy but it must be of an intellectual order. He does not like maudlin sympathy. He sees this as emotional silliness and pays it scant attention. What Gemini seeks is an intellectual sympathy that can reach out to him in a rational way.

Mark is a 16-year-old Gemini whose mother feels that there is a communication gap between them. When he has difficulties at school, Mark is reluctant to tell her about them. Yet, he is more than willing to confide in his father. Mark's mother tends to resent this, which causes occasional tension in the husband-wife relationship. The problem is that Mark's mother is guilty of an emotional concern over her teenage son's problems, rather than his successes, while his father offers him genuine understanding about his problems and admiration for what he is good at. Being a true Gemini, Mark responds to his father's more positive and more helpful approach and rejects the way his mother approaches him. Gemini wants sympathy, not advice.

A Gemini youngster is not a good listener and often resents suggestion. He wants you to see things from his point of view, not the other way around. If you confront him with an opposite or conflicting viewpoint, you will make little headway. No matter how practical or sensible your advice may be, it will fall on deaf Gemini ears. Clever sympathizing is an effective channel of communication with a Gemini youngster and a wise parent will use it to advantage.

Remember that Gemini is basically an egotist and the I-factor must always be taken into consideration. The best motivation is through the first-person pronoun. Gemini is a wonderful sign, versatile, and clever, but it is also egocentric. Perhaps this is the reason Gemini detests isolation—it feels that nobody should be denied the pleasure of its company!

146

CANCER

Nancy is just about everybody's favorite at school. She's quiet and tries very hard to please her teachers. This 13-year-old rarely makes trouble in the classroom and seems to be a conscientious student of better-than-average ability.

Imagine my surprise, at a PTA meeting, when Nancy's parents told me that at home she is an exceptionally moody child. One day she will be full of life and good spirits and suddenly her mood will change and she will become sulky and complaining. These changes seem to take place for no obvious reason. When scolded, according to her parents, Nancy stops talking and stays to herself. After a quarrel with a friend, this is also her pattern. It seems to be her way of showing hurt. She loves to dwell on some minor slight or imagined injustice at home and turns these things into major issues causing a great deal of unpleasantness at home. How is it, her parents asked, that these qualities don't seem to make themselves evident at school?

After checking her birthday and determining that she is a Cancerian, I could only explain to her parents that their daughter is a typical Moonchild. Like many Cancerians she has a soft, round, moon face and a motherly interest in others. She is very sympathetic with other children and will share their troubles. They often look to her for help and advice and seem to sense her maternal warmth.

Nancy is extremely sensitive. She has imagined hurts and dreamed-up injuries. She makes mountains out of molehills and experiences some difficulties with her friends because of this trait. There is seldom a time when she is on speaking terms with everyone. Fortunately, her spats do not last too long and she forgives easily—if the *other* person apologizes!

Despite this sensitivity, Nancy is a warm, engaging child. She is pretty and can be utterly charming. She is especially responsive to younger children and enjoys caring for them. Occasionally, she babysits for a neighbor and has been praised for her ability and competence.

Nancy is deeply attached to her parents and gives them her complete devotion, except for her periods of moodiness. She is certainly daddy's little darling and loves to be with him. She helps her mother with the household chores and even prepares some of the family meals. She is very domestic and enjoys interior decorating and rearranging the furniture.

Sometimes, the moodiness of our children is something we can do little about—except to learn to live with it and help them to learn to live with it. At least if we recognize this kind of Cancerian personality, we can spot the mood coming on and try to ease the problems it may cause, recognizing that it is only a temporary condition soon to be replaced with warmth and pleasantness.

Nancy's parents began to realize that they had a very unique child whose moods simply had to be understood.

At the next PTA meeting, Nancy's mother confided in me that our little chat had resulted in her pressing Nancy less when the moods arose and, in turn, this lack of pressure seemed to have a strong effect in lessening the moods.

Disciplining and Motivating Cancer

Cancer is a sensitive, sympathetic, and tenacious sign. The true Cancerian is able not only to project emotion but to reflect emotion. This sign can make others sense the intensity of its feelings as well as its ability to share deeply the emotional intensity of others. It is a giving and taking sign, always adapting to an emotional climate.

As a result, the Cancerian child is one of the few children

of the Zodiac who will respond to words alone. Let Cancer know how much his poor behavior disturbs and even hurts you. A few well-chosen words work wonders with a Cancer child. If you can effectively project your concern and your loving disapproval, your Cancerian child will respond with cooperation and enthusiasm. Assure him of your love and of your hope that he will respond to it by behaving positively. You may even expect tears and assurances of "I'm sorry." Cancer is innately sensitive and will respond to your every word. Never raise your voice with Cancer. A quiet, firm tone is all you need. If you scold or your voice level rises, Cancer will feel rejected. Gentle firmness is the key.

Parents must be extremely careful not to subject their Cancer child to any injudicious or harsh discipline. If so, a Cancerian child's reactions may be out of proportion to the situation. A Cancerian child is deeply sensitive and strong discipline may engender strong resentment. He may forgive but he never forgets! Severity and harshness are rarely effective with Cancer. Although they may bring temporary results, their long-term implications are quite damaging.

In disciplining a Cancer, a parent need do only two things. The first step is to reassure Cancer of your love and the second is to convince him of your disappointment. Both these things can be done with words, and the proper words at the proper times will control Cancer. This sign needs emotional communication and emotional security. He craves parental love and approval and will go to any length to secure it. A wise parent will use this native longing for effective control and training.

Some discipline problems may be caused by the flair for drama which the children of this sign have, sometimes to the point of absurdity.

Ten-year-old John got the notion that he was an adopted child. He told his playmates that he didn't know who his real parents were but that some day he would find them. He played the role of an abandoned child to the hilt, finally demanding that his parents tell him the brutal truth. Fortunately, his mother understood and helped him return to reality.

Some Cancerian children develop imaginary illnesses and imaginary defects. Fourteen-year-old Lorraine played at losing her sight. She demanded glasses, even successfully convinced her teachers that her vision was defective. Finally, her parents took her to an ophthalmologist who found 20/20 vision in both eyes. This dramatic episode cost Lorraine's parents over 30 dollars! A prudent parent of a Cancer investigates any sudden development with scrutiny. It may be real but it may also be just an imaginary flair for getting the center of the stage with drama.

Since Cancer is motivated through the emotions, Cancer is one of the easiest victims of clever advertising. If you want to motivate your Cancerian child, then you must advertise your product. Build in appeal and attraction and you will get a sympathetic response. If you want improved scholastic achievement, for example, associate it with parental love and approbation. Cancer will work for better grades if he thinks he is working to please a loved one. Your approval and your affection are very important to the Cancerian child.

In dealing with Cancerian children, remember that they are the victims and not the masters of their emotions. They are sentimental and moody. Like their ruling planet, the moon, they are ever-changing. They move from one mood to the next. They are also tender and warm, capable of wonderful imagery and deep feeling. With Cancer, the heart rules the head. These are the characteristics that provide roadways to the inner self. Although Cancer may rationalize, his essential message will be emotional and his theme will be an intensity of feeling.

In either disciplining or motivating a Cancerian youngster,

joy, sorrow, hope, compassion, and despair will be your means of communication. As a Cancerian friend of mine once said, "I can be talked into anything!" This is the secret of working with Cancer.

LEO

Herbie, a 14-year-old, was spending all his allowance—and then some—on buying ice cream and other goodies for his schoolmates. One day his mother called me and complained. She was finding it impossible to cope with his incessant demands for entertainment money and asked if I could help.

I checked on Herbie's sun sign. He is a true Leo. He even walks like a king, strutting about with his head held high. There are times when he even seemed to be looking down his nose.

I discovered that Herbie is generous to a fault in many ways. He can never do enough for his friends and always repays a favor promptly. He cannot tolerate pettiness or self-ishness.

Herbie is an extrovert and loves to be with people. His one social problem is his tendency to decide that he doesn't have to listen to his playmates. Under certain circumstances, Herbie turns off and his playmates sense his aloofness. This sometimes happens during a festive occasion. Once, at a birthday party, Herbie suddenly decided that he was above it all and stopped playing the party games. He can assume a look of complete disdain that is almost a sneer. He does the same thing in school should the lesson bore him or the teacher displease him. Thankfully, it does not last too long.

Herbie is a very competent student and likes to study. He is successful in school and usually gets good report cards. Given the proper motivation, Herbie can make the honor roll. His parents have learned to praise him for his efforts. Herbie loves praise and compliments.

Herbie has a few selected good friends and spends most of his time with them. Although liked by the other children, it is Herbie who decides who will be with Herbie.

I invited him to my office for a chat.

"Herbie," I said, "your Mother tells me that you're trying to be the Aristotle Onassis of this school. You're spending too much of your Dad's money on the other students. It's fine to be generous, but this is ridiculous."

We chatted about the fact that there are many ways to show friendship, but I made it clear that it was practically impossible to buy it. I pointed out his obligations to his parents as well as to his friends. Our Leo was quite willing to listen; most Leos have a sense of family responsibility, too.

By the time the conversation was over, Herbie was convinced that his generosity had to be tempered with prudence.

I was so pleased with myself that I considered taking him out and buying him an ice cream cone!

Disciplining and Motivating Leo

Proud, royal Leo is the king sign of the Zodiac. Like his symbol, the lion, he is domineering and authoritative with a fierceness that can intimidate and a roar that can frighten. He has an unquenchable thirst for glory and power and asserts his kingship at every opportunity. The parents of a Leo know this royal nature only too well!

This is the hardest sign of the Zodiac to control. The Leo child holds himself above everything and everybody. He looks upon any disciplinary measure with disdain and he rejects any authority other than his own. As Leo is never wrong, he feels that any punishment is totally unjust. Leo is certain that he is incapable of a shortcoming and convinced that he is without flaw. Never, never argue with your

Leo child or attempt to convince him of guilt. You will waste your words! His mind was already made up before you started speaking. Spanking Leo or depriving him of some pleasure will also be ineffective discipline. He will just consider himself a victim of your ignorance and your unwillingness to listen. It is not unlike Leos to accept discipline stoically yet reject all that it stands for.

Probably the most effective disciplinary measure is based on Leo's intense pride. Leo does not like to be ignored. He must always be in center stage and part of the action. Ignore him and you reach him. Cutting him off from your awareness will disturb him and reach beneath his egotism. The Pennsylvania Dutch call this treatment "shunning." You "shun" a person by removing him from your consciousness. When Leo is "shunned" he is punished. Try simply failing to respond to him for a while. He won't be able to take your silent treatment for long. Within a short time, your Leo child will be begging for attention and willing to pay the price.

Fred is a Leo and this technique works with him. When there has been an infraction of some rule or misdeed, Fred is informed of what he has done. Then he is courteously but definitely ignored. Usually he finally agrees to cooperate. Of course, I am certain that he still thinks he has been innocently persecuted! A Leo dies hard!

Leo, like the cat family, purrs when he is gently treated. But don't ruffle his fur! In motivating Leo cooperation, it is important to stroke the fur in the right way. Appeal to his egotism and to his pride. Leo loves a challenge and an opportunity to prove himself. He achieves success through a strong desire for superiority. Leo does not work to please others. He works to prove and please himself. Assure him of his ability and feed his vanity. Many parents of Leo children would find parenthood easier if they stroked the fur rather than rubbed it.

It is easy to lose your cool with a Leo when you wish that

something would happen to deflate his ego. Remember that he is a product of his sun sign and may be unable to control these inclinations. Understand them and take pride in the many brilliant and superior qualities this sign displays. A Leo child is a joy and a pleasure once you understand his pride and his dominant nature.

Despite his pride and his regality, Leo is capable of moodiness. Frequently a Leo child will fall into a mood of dark depression. He may become dejected and feel that there can be no success in his life. He may suddenly decide that school is a complete failure and that he may as well give up completely. Or his dejection may be social. He may decide that nobody likes him and that he has no true friends. This moodiness of Leo is a curious thing as it seems so out of character. It is at this time that your Leo child needs a double dose of ego-building and nourishment for his tarnished vanity. Don't agree with him! Be positive instead. Humor him. Assure him. Reinforce his damaged image. His discontent and dissatisfaction will be short-lived if your support is close at hand.

For the most part, a Leo child needs little motivation. His sun sign characteristics offer sufficient inner motivation to bring positive results both in school and in society. This is a hopeful and confident sign, endowed with determination and a strong will. Your role in raising a Leo youngster will be more in guiding him than in motivating him, and in helping him to use his sun sign qualities wisely and well.

VIRGO

Wally's mother dropped by my office one day to complain that her nine-year-old son was being given too much homework. "He's never got any time to play like the other kids," she said.

I shook my head. "Wally is a very bright boy and should

be able to do his homework in plenty of time to allow for as much recreation as he really wants. There must be some other explanation," I said. "Let me check into it."

That same day, wandering through the library, I noticed Wally sitting at a table, his nose buried in a book, during the outside-activity time. Next day, I checked the library and found him there again.

In these days, when it is so difficult to get youngsters to read books at all, I was reluctant to make any move to take him out of the library. I investigated Wally's records and found that he was a Virgo, a serious, conscientious student with a quick intellect. He even looks studious, usually frowning in deep thought. His eyes betray his intellectual interests.

Wally's teachers comment on his intense patience. He can wait for the right moment to act regardless of the time involved. His mind is set and his determination is remarkable. Once committed to a project, he steers a steady course.

Wally is very much a perfectionist and wants everything just so. His bed must be properly made before he will sleep, and his food must be carefully prepared. Not just anything will do for Wally! He can be very demanding and lets you know about it.

Wally has a remarkable memory for detail. He never seems to forget the smallest thing. He remembers well and carefully records everything that happens for future reference. This has its negative aspect. His mother complains that bad habits, thought to be broken, return. He is almost dogged in his involvement.

Wally is a typical Virgo in his relationships with others. He seems to have a heart of steel and can turn his affection on or off at will. He is more ruled by his head than his heart. His friends are appreciated but seldom missed. Even with his parents, Wally demonstrates the same seeming objectivity.

I talked to Wally's Physical Education teacher and discovered that he refused to take part in the games. Athletic activities simply didn't interest him. I talked to his father and discovered that even during the summer vacations, Wally's parents had to force him to go out and play—he'd rather spend his time in contemplation or reading.

Obviously, it was going to be a difficult job convincing this typical Virgo to change his ways—just a bit, anyway. So, I asked him to my office and we discussed the situation.

"It's a waste of time!" he exclaimed about baseball. "It's so childish!"

I tried one of my typical Cancer ploys. "It's not as simple as you think!" I said. "I bet you don't know how major league batting averages are figured out!"

Not only did he not know, he had no idea there was such a thing. So, I asked him, as a favor to me, to look at the sports pages and try to figure out the mathematical formula.

Within a couple of days, he had the answer. And he kept watching. Within a month he was a baseball fan. And very soon, the Physical Education instructor was reporting to me that Wally was showing some interest in games, and even taking part himself.

It's unlikely that Wally will grow up to be the Mickey Mantle of the next generation. Nobody was trying to accomplish that anyway. And it's unlikely that Virgo Wally will even give up much of his valued library time. Nobody wants that either. But it is likely that our understanding of what makes Virgo tick will result in a slightly more rounded, better adjusted Wally.

Disciplining and Motivating Virgo

Virgo is a sign of service and industry. The Virgo gives of himself and of his resources. He finds satisfaction in being of assistance to others and his strength and ability are dedicated to his serious approach to life. Virgo classifies, organizes, and discriminates. This hard-working child of the Zodiac can be trusted with responsibility. Virgos can become so wrapped up in duty that they appear cold and aloof. They usually live according to the letter of the law and see things as black or white. There are few shades of gray and their justice is rarely tempered with mercy.

With these sun sign characteristics, parents are not likely to have much trouble with Virgo children. They will find them conscientious, industrious, and responsible. Generally speaking, Virgo gets along well with adults and is more than willing to accept adult standards of behavior. A Virgo child conforms to rules and regulations and seldom questions the decisions of those in authority. He can be taught good manners easily and he will often undertake household responsibilities without being asked. The same seriousness manifests itself in the classroom. Virgo takes school and schoolwork seriously and uses great care in completing his school assignments.

This is not to say, however, that Virgo never needs discipline. On the contrary, but you will spend the larger part of your time dealing with small, insignificant incidents. Often, just a strong warning will bring Virgo back into line. Your Virgo youngster will seldom become involved in situations requiring major discipline. This sign can make ripples but does not like to make waves.

According to one parent of a Virgo child, there are times when you worry and wish that they would do something wrong just to reassure you that they are normal children. Some Virgos can be so totally well-behaved that they cause concern.

Richard is a Virgo and he is so well-behaved that he is disliked by the other children and mistrusted by some adults. He is serious, studious, and organized. His attitude is so adult that his aunt calls him "our family's old man." Keep in mind that the Virgo nature places immense value on accuracy, method, and duty. It has a certain puritanical quality that can irritate less serious signs. Virgos can be witty and gracious but they are always industrious. The head rules the heart and frivolity has little function in a methodical existence.

Motivating Virgo is a relatively simple matter. Tell them what to do and they will do it, provided it is logically acceptable, legal, and moral. This sign gives ungrudgingly of its strength to please and serve others. It needs little motivation beyond its own native spirit. Nevertheless, make no excessive or unreasonable demands. Virgo can say no and mean it! They will give, please, serve, and care, but they will not have these talents abused. Don't take advantage of them. Too often, parents of Virgo children get so accustomed to their cooperation and add straws that break the camel's back. Remember that there are limitations to anyone's endurance.

Rachel's parents were used to good report cards and teacher praise. She was an average student and worked right up to her ability. There was little more she could do, but her standard made her parents believe she could do more, and they began to demand perfection. They wanted the B's to become A's and the A's to become A pluses. They couldn't understand it when Rachel suddenly stopped trying. Her grades dropped and her attitude toward school became negative. She was saying no and meaning it. Virgo can be excessively stubborn if pushed too far.

Virgo is a highly practical sign, which values the useful and the proved. It does not expect lavish praise and seldom gives it to others. At times, Virgos can be cantankerous and irritable. This is often caused by the frustrations involved in their rigid approach to daily life. They can have a depressing effect on those around them because of their dreary dedication to duty. They should be encouraged to participate in social activities and to indulge in periods of relaxation. Parents of Virgo children should spend most of their time tempering their metallic spirits and softening their rigid ways.

LIBRA

A group of militant students were demanding the right to establish specific time limits on homework for each subject in the school's curriculum! The teachers were adamant—this constituted an outrageous encroachment on their rights and responsibilities as teachers. Not only would they refuse to accede to the student demands—they would refuse even to discuss them. It was an impasse. It was not merely a generation gap, it was a chasm.

Then, along came Doris—a Libran. A girl with gentleness and poise and charm. A girl with both feet firmly planted in her own generation—but with her hands reaching out in a friendly gesture to the older generation.

With typical Libran maturity beyond her years, Doris was able to speak with both groups. She was able to convince the teachers that the students might not have the right to set homework standards, but that they certainly had the right to discuss such a thing. And she was able to convince the students that, if nothing else, the open discussion of such a matter constituted a great step forward for them. In typical Libran fashion, Doris was able to turn the potential disaster into an academic love-in.

Doris' charming manner pleases just about everybody; she enjoys a large circle of friends. She is closely attached to her parents and is considered a dutiful daughter. However, she is somewhat jealous of her younger brother and at times resents the intrusion of this new family member. She carries the same attitude with her outside of her home. Doris seems to resent any intrusion on her friendship or on the time she can spend with her friends. In all her relationships, she demonstrates a possessiveness typical of her sun sign.

Doris' parents provided her with a piano and piano lessons while she was in fifth grade. She is now an accomplished musician and plays the organ at church. She loves music and interprets it beautifully.

In high school, Doris is a good student and achieves well. She is precise and exacting in her written work and plans her assignments carefully. Like most Librans, she is excessively time-conscious. She wears a watch and checks the time frequently. Her favorite expressions are "in due time" and "as time passes."

Doris likes fine things and enjoys the luxuries of life. While quite young, her mother taught her how to sew and embroider. Doris has made many lovely items. Her mother marvels at her ability to stitch so finely and so skillfully. She likes quality clothing and dresses in good taste.

Doris plans to continue with her musical training after graduation and has already been accepted by a leading conservatory.

If the younger generation is going to manage to overcome the communications problem, chances are that Librans like Doris will play an important part in that maneuver.

Disciplining and Motivating Libra

Libra is the sign of balance and is an alert, just, and affectionate sign. Many astrologers consider Libra the finest sign in the Zodiac. Librans are alive, alert, and resourceful. They have a sense of propriety that is enviable and a good humor that is a joy to behold. They often have great charm and gentle ways. They are cheerful, optimistic, and encouraging.

The positive Libran is patient and kind. He is scrupulously honorable and exceedingly considerate. The negative Libran can waste time over details and hedge about decisions. He can be unknowingly inconsiderate and use his Libran charm to get his own way and satisfy his own desires.

Clearly, the Libran child can be a charmer or a terror depending on how he uses his Libran qualities. The positive Libran gives little trouble. The negative Libran can lead his parents on a merry chase. Many a Libran child can turn on his charm like household water and use it to his own advantage. A quick Libran smile and a ready Libran laugh has averted many a parental confrontation.

As Libra likes to plan carefully and thoroughly enjoys the anticipation of future pleasure, you can use this characteristic to guide him. Denying Libra something that he has planned will bring about cooperation. With most children, punishment must be immediate to be effective. This is not true with Libra. Informing him that he is to be denied a future outing or a planned excursion is enough.

Librans are usually intelligent and learn easily. Repetition is not often necessary.

Libran children sometimes manifest a confusion of interests. This often causes parental concern. The Libran child may move from interest to interest and seem slow in starting. He may procrastinate and waste time worrying over details. If your Libran child shows indications of this tendency, help him to overcome it. Don't compound the situation with scoldings or impatience. Help him by making decisions for him and leading him into a sense of self-security. With many Libran children, you may have to take over the driver's seat and steer for them. These children are often thankful and relieved that you are there to lean on.

The majority of Libran children are easily motivated. Being under the sign of balance, they know how to live wisely and well. They have a natural instinct for sanity and practicality and will make decisions accordingly. Librans seem to sense the right thing to do and the right time to do it. They are appreciative of life and responsive to the blessings of life. They have a certain intuition that guides them into a wholesome and sincere philosophy.

It is comforting to know that the native Libran wants to live in harmony with those around him. He prizes their approbation and appreciates their concerns. Their efforts in this direction may not always be laudable but their intent is sincere. Parents of Librans will find their suggestions falling on open ears and their guidance followed.

Some Librans have a restlessness about them and a tendency to dream in favor of practicality. These children must be kept occupied and urged to persevere in their undertakings. But most are extraordinarily balanced and instinctively know how to pursue the good life.

SCORPIO

Marianne is a member of a large family. Six of the children attended my school at the same time. That's why I was a bit surprised when her mother called to ask why it was that all the children except Marianne had brought home report cards to be signed.

I said I would check on it, and soon found Marianne's card on file. It had been returned with her father's signature —obviously forged!

I decided to investigate Marianne's case a bit further before I confronted her.

She has dark, penetrating eyes typical of Scorpio and usually she reveals an instinct for knowing the right time to act and the proper moment for decision. She demonstrates this both in school and at play.

Marianne is a very practical child and is relentless in her pursuits. Once she has committed herself to a project, it gets her complete and undivided attention. She leaves nothing to chance and can maneuver situations to her advantage.

Typical of this sign, Marianne is an ingenious and self-controlled little girl. She will rarely discuss any plans with either her parents or her companions. True to her Scorpio nature, Marianne is secretive and sometimes evasive.

When Marianne quarrels with her playmates, she tends to hold her grievance too long. She forgives but she does not forget and her parents observe that she enjoys retaliating. They have tried to discourage this unfortunate inclination.

In school, Marianne is a fair student with great ability for concentration. Her teachers remark about her powers of concentration and note how she can become completely absorbed in anything that interests her. She loves to read and can lose herself in a story.

Marianne is a suspicious child and never quite trusts her playmates' motives. She will often voice her suspicions at home and her parents are concerned about this characteristic.

I talked to Marianne's mother again and learned that when report card time arrived, the father has all the children line up and show their grades to him. I was appalled!

This was obviously a terrible invasion of privacy for any self-respecting Scorpio. Marianne undoubtedly resented this ordeal of publicly unveiling her report card in the living room ceremony!

Aside from the fact that this procedure violated Scorpio sensibilities, the practice is a poor one under any circumstance. Every youngster deserves a certain amount of privacy regarding his scholastic achievements—or non-achievements.

Marianne was reprimanded for the forgery, but so were her parents. And, next report period, when the cruel inspection procedure was eliminated, Marianne brought her signed report card back to school with the authentic signature of her properly chastened Dad.

Disciplining and Motivating Scorpio

The sign of Scorpio is energetic, passionate, and determined. It is a sign of strong likes and dislikes and extremes of intensity. Whatever is at hand is done with energy and passion. Scorpio courage is steadfast and the Scorpio will is like steel.

When a Scorpio child is bad, he is very bad. He throws himself wholeheartedly into mischief and misconduct. Allowed to go unchecked, your Scorpio child can become a Scorpio terror! It is most important that Scorpio children are properly trained and carefully checked. They need structure and firmness. A Scorpio child will take advantage of parental weakness or indecision. Not only are consistency of discipline and expectations imperative in controlling this sign, but insistency is also. There are times when Scorpio cooperation must be demanded.

To compound the situation, Scorpio has a certain Spartan quality that can accept disciplinary measures stoically. No matter what the form or intensity, Scorpio can take it. It can be a frustrating experience to spank a Scorpio and find that not a tear is shed. There are times when you can actually see a Scorpio child brace himself for correction with an almost brazen determination not to react. He doesn't mind isolation or deprivation and he has a high tolerance for physical discomfort. Scorpio is a difficult sign to correct, as parents of Scorpio children can attest.

A word of warning. Never send Scorpio to his room as punishment. This sign loves to be alone and isolation is frequently welcomed. There may be times when Scorpio has to be isolated for the good of others, but never use isolation as a threat or as a means of discipline.

The Scorpio nature realizes that discipline is a part of life and must be accepted. More than any other sun sign, Scorpio accepts discipline without resentment. This is what makes disciplining this sign so impossible.

There are some students of astrology who claim that Scorpio cannot be controlled by outside forces. They say that the only true Scorpio discipline is self-discipline. With a will of iron and an abnormal determination, only a Scorpio can control a Scorpio. If this be true, then the parents of Scorpio children must help them develop inner controls and self-discipline. This must be inaugurated in the cradle and developed through the growing years. It may be much too late to teach self-discipline to a teenager. There are times when resignation is wisdom and we must learn to live with our mistakes. If properly trained, Scorpio can have a deep seriousness, self-command, and sincerity. It is an intensely virile sign and can demonstrate a strong masculine control, but it must be directed and guided if it is to develop its positive nature. Scorpio can be as stern with himself as he can be with others.

One of the chief difficulties in raising a Scorpio child is teaching him to control his passions. His passions are stronger than other children's and he can rouse himself to intensities of hatred, anger, jealousy, and rebellion. Scorpio doesn't just dislike a teacher or a playmate, he hates. When aroused, Scorpio doesn't make ripples, he makes waves. Prudent parents will channel this intensity of passion into legitimate expression. Scorpio can be a reformer or an angry young man. It is vital that he get angry over the right things. His passion can be a tremendous force in good motivation. Unleashed in the proper direction, the aggressive Scorpio can change the world. His strength can protect the weak and his endurance can overcome any obstacle.

Parents of Scorpio girls should remember that this is a virile, masculine sign and that even in our age of uni-sex and non-discrimination, the Scorpio girl finds it hard to accept the limitations imposed by her sex. Scorpio girls often are tomboys and some of them secretly wish that they had been born boys. Their drive and discipline make Scorpio women great leaders when they wish to be, spotless housekeepers, excellent cooks, devoted mothers, and passionate mates.

Scorpio has courage, resolution, and fierce independence. The real challenge of Scorpio parenthood is direction, not imposition. Controlling and motivating your Scorpio child is more an art than a science.

SAGITTARIUS

Andy is a regular Agnew of the schoolyard. He is forever putting his foot in his mouth, with blunt statements or hard-to-take criticism.

He was hospitalized in the fourth grade after being pushed off the jungle gym. He'd called an older boy Fatty and down he went! In the fifth grade, he told his teacher that he didn't like her because she was a poor instructor. This paid off in poor grades and resentment. Now, in the sixth grade, he was in my office for using improper language in the classroom.

"May I leave the room to go urinate?" he'd asked.

Of course, the whole class had embarrassed hysterics and the teacher marched him directly to my office.

"Why did you feel it was necessary to explain in detail the purpose of your visit to the restroom?" I asked.

"Gee," he said, "I was only telling the truth! It's not as if I said I had to go take a. . . ."

I interrupted quickly. "Certainly, it was truthful, Andy.

But the complete truth is not always called for—or even necessary. Sometimes, when offered without reason, it can be cruel—or, in this case, disruptive." There was no question in my mind that I was dealing with a painfully honest Sagittarian.

Andy is an independent, outgoing youngster who loves to talk and get involved. In school, he experiences some difficulty in paying attention and keeping still. He is always out of his seat or squirming around. His teachers complain about this constantly.

Andy is always talking about a new project. In one year, he was a paperboy, a yard helper, a window washer, and an errand boy. He has lots of ideas about earning money but very little persistence. He tires quickly of a venture and seeks out new schemes.

Andy does not like school and declares his dislike often. His work is sloppy and poorly done and he has responded to only one teacher. In fourth grade, Andy had a male teacher who seemed to reach him. This was the only year that Andy received a decent report card. Usually his report cards are poor and invoke his parents' ire. He has ability but fails to use it.

But, back to the problem at hand.

"What should I have said, sir?" he asked in seeming innocence.

"You know very well, Andy," I answered. "You should simply have asked if you might leave the room, just as all the other children do. Imposing your own brand of honesty on everybody is sometimes more harmful than helpful."

"Sir," Andy interrupted. "I don't want to seem discourteous, but you'd better let me leave the room right now before I wet my pants!"

I let him go quickly. After all, Sagittarians are known to be doers!

Disciplining and Motivating Sagittarius

Sagittarius is an impulsive, candid, and curious sign. Its symbol is the archer, shooting arrows into the air and aiming at distant targets. It is a sign that is not complex in its emotional nature. Sagittarian motives are easily understood and readily exposed. It is a straightforward sign, free of deceit, and strangely transparent of soul.

Sagittarius is also a "talk" sign. It responds to logic and conversational learning. Socrates was born under this sun sign and everything about him discloses the Sagittarian nature.

This sign is a natural for child psychology because it is as anxious to understand its behavior as you are. Help your Sagittarian youngster to analyze his conduct and to understand the motives and reasons underlying his actions. And it won't be too difficult for you to understand because your Sagittarian child is so guileless and uncomplicated. Sagittarius needs to know why he has done something and, once he understands, he will act favorably on this knowledge. Words are your most effective control when dealing with this sign. Talk to him, explain, exemplify, analyze, sympathize! This child wants to know why he has misbehaved and why it was wrong.

Tony is a Sagittarian and will often talk with himself. In conversation it is not unusual to hear him analyze and dissect his behavior. "I guess I did that because I was a little jealous." "I wonder why I did that—maybe I resented what she said." These are typical self-analytic remarks that pepper Tony's speech. When you offer to participate in this analysis, Tony is quite receptive. He enjoys knowing about himself and is pleased that you share his interest. One rarely has to scold a Sagittarian youngster. They are too open and too willing to change. They will accept your criticism and act on it.

This is not to say that a very young Sagittarian might not benefit from occasional strong discipline. There are many times in the growing process when the seat is the door to learning. But if you are still spanking your 12-year-old Sagittarian, then you have missed the boat. By the age of reason and rationality, Sagittarius can be effectively controlled through conversation and discussion. Of course, this takes time and interest and there are lazy parents. The path of least resistance is not always the best path to take. One parent confessed, "I don't have the time to understand him!" It is regrettable that a sign so susceptible to words was made the victim of indifference.

Sagittarian motivation is again a matter of intellect and rationality. Once he knows the reasons and all the whys and wherefores, the Sagittarian child will cooperate. To demand his cooperation will be futile. Sagittarius often resents a direct assertion of authority. Rather, persuade him that his cooperation is the best course of action. Sagittarius accepts and selects premises that have been cleverly presented. It is a sign that values common sense and it will rarely go against it. A Sagittarian teenager, if exposed to the current anti-smoking campaign, will probably not smoke. It is not the scare he responds to, it is the logic.

In dealing with your young Sagittarian, it is imperative to answer his questions and to administer discipline with fairness and logic. It is equally important to admit that you don't know or that you were wrong. The Sagittarian child respects honesty and frankness and certainly expects it of those he loves and admires. He is very willing to submit to parental wisdom but he may test it from time to time. "Why?" is his favorite and most frequent question. He can be exasperating and his questions can become tiresome. He is outspoken and often undiplomatic, but the way to reach him and to hold him is through reason and logic.

CAPRICORN

While walking through the school hallway, I noticed 13-year-old Chet using the public telephone.

"Do you have permission?" I asked.

He nodded.

"And who are you calling?" I asked. Chet was supposed to be in his first class.

"The police!" he said. He hung up and proceeded to rejoin his class.

I contacted the police station and, to my amazement, discovered that Chet had informed the chief that the father of one of his classmates had violated the speed limit in front of the school!

Only the day before, I knew that the lesson had concerned civic duties and the teacher had explained the concept of citizen arrests. Obviously, this Capricorn child felt that he was only doing his duty!

Chet is a perfect Capricorn. Perfect could be his middle name! Everything he does is proper and he is sometimes too good to be true. His parents have no complaints about his behavior and feel that they have been blessed.

In school, Chet is equally as well-behaved. He tries to please his teacher and is conscientious about his assignments. He rarely violates a rule or regulation and is often chosen as the class monitor during the teacher's absence. There is some resentment against him from the other children, especially the boys.

He is a Boy Scout and takes scouting as seriously as everything else. He works diligently for merit badges and is now a first class scout. He was elected the leader of his scout patrol and the scoutmaster has commented on his leadership ability.

Chet tends to be somewhat scrappy with the other children. He is sure that he is right and insists on their cooperation. He likes to quote rules and regulations and, when given authority, makes a hard task master.

Chet is prone to some sneakiness. Even his teachers have noticed this. He will talk behind their back or misbehave when they are out of sight. At home, he does the same thing with his parents. His mother has caught him at this on several occasions.

Altogether, Chet is a perfect son, a perfect student, and a perfect scout. He has persistence and stamina and works with diligence and earnestness. In his adult life, Chet will probably be an upright citizen and a worldly success.

But right now I was faced with an immediate situation of avoiding any censure of Chet for his behavior but still making it clear that some discretion had to be used.

The police chief was very understanding and suggested that I inform Chet that he might have been mistaken in his estimate of the actual speed of the car. Also, the citizen arrest must be physically accomplished by the citizen, not the police.

I asked Chet to visit me at the end of the day and we discussed all of the details of citizen's arrest. He agreed that perhaps he had been a little hasty and that his evidence was not exactly overwhelming. On this basis, he agreed not to pursue the matter. But he was very pleased by my approval of his high level of civic responsibility.

We said goodbye and Chet started for home. I retrieved my car from the parking lot. Capricorns! I thought to myself, as I drove down the street.

You can bet I drove slowly as I passed Chet!

Capricorn is a sign that takes life seriously and is a firm believer in tradition and authority. It is a persevering, reserved, and proper sign. The Capricorn is ambitious, adaptable, and extraordinarily able to accept an environment. It has an instinctive understanding of society and a strong political sense. The goat ascending the mountain is the symbol of this sign and it is indicative of Capricorn's determination to follow the upward path. "Ever onward, ever upward" might well be the motto of the native son of Capricorn.

Disciplining and Motivating Capricorn

The parent of a Capricorn child is lucky. You will rarely, if ever, have cause to discipline a Capricorn youngster. This sign is so eager to please that it will hesitate before doing anything that might hurt a loved one or displease authority. In its constant desire to extend courtesy and consideration, Capricorn calls into play a tremendous amount of self-control. The typical Capricorn child is scrupulously aware of rules and regulations, and places high value on conformity. Should some disciplinary measure be called for, a simple and direct demonstration of your displeasure will be most effective. A disapproving glance or a stern reprimand is all that is ever necessary to control the Capricorn.

Capricorn is well behaved, but he can go astray. When he does, it will be in secret and behind your back. Your approval is constantly before him and, even in his misconduct, he is painfully aware of it. This often drives a Capricorn youngster into clandestine misbehavior and secret sin. The Capricorn youngster can be a perfect angel but a secret devil. He is always aware of adult approbation and the desires of authority figures. This tendency can lead to some undesirable traits and should be guarded against. Urge your Capricorn child to be open and above-board, and when you discover that he isn't, let Capricorn know your displeasure at both the deed and the manner in which it was done.

One of Capricorn's serious faults is the desire to meddle in the affairs of others. Capricorn children are the ones most likely to go through mother's dresser drawers or poke around daddy's desk. They love to stick their noses into places and things that do not concern them. This can prove to be somewhat irritating. Henry loves to answer the phone and his conversation can be quite embarrassing. His older sister has complained that he asks her boyfriends embarrassing questions. He has opened family mail and enjoys eavesdropping on adult conversation. These are all manifestations of his Capricorn desire to influence and manage others. Hopefully, as he grows older he will learn to control it and direct this tendency into more acceptable actions.

The most effective motivation for a Capricorn child is an appeal to authority, tradition, or social standards. He reveres the past, he respects heritage and he renders homage to those in control. Although other children resent the records of older brothers and sisters and dislike being reminded of their achievements, this is not true of Capricorn. This sign has great appreciation for the success of those who have gone before him and is quite willing to acknowledge the attainment of others.

Often, Capricorn children will respond to the example of others in their family and try to share in their success. A Capricorn child will have a sincere respect for his family's social position or academic record. This youngster does not reject the paths that others have followed and the trails that have been blazed. His admiration for those who have preceded him is tremendous. He is grateful for their guidance and embraces their ambition as his own.

The parent of a Capricorn should capitalize on this characteristic and use it to advantage. They should realize that

Capricorn children want to succeed and welcome the challenge of good example.

One of Capricorn's potential vices is a tendency toward snobbism. A Capricorn child may become so smug over his conservatism and love of conformity that he may hold other points of view in contempt. Frequently a Capricorn child falls into the habit of prefacing everything with "my teacher says" or "my mother says." This can lead to an insidious snobbery and cause trouble with peer relationships. Not many children like to be reminded constantly of what teacher says or what mother thinks.

In this respect, Christopher is a typical Capricorn. Only in the seventh grade, he has already developed a superior and condescending attitude. He looks down on those who will not conform or who have trouble in relating to adult behavior.

This Capricorn snobbery can assume many guises. At one time it is a groveling before those with rank and authority and at other times it is an irritating haughtiness. Wise parents of Capricorn children will make every effort to control this and to teach the Capricorn that not all people value the same things. What the Capricorn considers suitable and proper is often a matter of personal opinion. Capricorn is the sign of the good citizen but a good citizen respects the rights and opinions of others.

AQUARIUS

Jane burst into my office with a look of fury in her eyes. "You're an absolute racist!" she shouted. "And I'm going to report you to the Civil Liberties Union—and—and—the Black Panthers, too!"

I knew the reasons for Jane's outburst. Bruce, a black

174

student, had just been disciplined. Bruce, an intelligent but very emotional youngster, had stormed out of an American History class when the teacher brought up the subject of George Washington Carver and peanuts.

"I'm not going to sit here and listen to that honkie crap about one of the worst Uncle Toms of my race!" he'd shouted, completely disrupting the class.

Jane was currently involved in a big crush on Bruce. The relationship was typical of her Aquarian nature. Bruce should never be criticized, except by her. Bruce is always right, except perhaps when he happens to disagree with her. Aquarians have intense loyalty to both their friends and their own opinions!

Jane was born in early February and, like the members of her sign, she is outgoing and social. She enjoys being with other teenagers and likes nothing better than a birthday party or a summer outing. If given the choice, life would be one big party.

In school, Jane is a good student but has very pronounced likes and dislikes. Without too much reason, she dislikes history and me, the school principal. The former is "boring" and I am "dumb." Surprisingly, she gets good grades in history and I am very fond of her. But once Jane has made up her mind about something or somebody, it takes a long time to change it. She is much the same way with her classmates. She seems to decide instantly who will be liked and who will be disliked.

To those she likes, Jane is extremely loyal and constant. She will defend her friends and woe to anyone who attacks those closest to her—witness her reaction to my disciplining of Bruce.

Jane, like most Aquarians, loves to offer an opinion. She states it dogmatically and emphatically. This sometimes gets her into trouble with her teachers.

I've had much experience with Aquarians and I knew how to cope with Jane.

"Jane," I said calmly, "you may not agree with many of my more moderate opinions, but you certainly know I'm not a racist."

"No, I don't!" she insisted. "After all, the only thing Bruce did was say what's true!"

"First of all," I replied, "I'm not so sure that George Washington Carver was an Uncle Tom. But, even if he were, he still made a great impact on American society both with his scientific work and because he was one of the first modern blacks to capture the imagination of young people of his own race as well as the white race. And second of all, there's absolutely no excuse for Bruce's shouting in class and stalking out. If he honestly believes what he says, then the thing to do would be to open up that discussion in class and make sure that his point of view is understood—and appreciated."

"But Bruce says that the whole school system is racist and, as long as American History is taught with white-oriented textbooks, there will never be any improvement," she insisted.

"If that is the case—and I question it—don't you think that both you and Bruce should be fighting to change the textbooks rather than abandoning students to the books that you feel are objectionable?" I asked.

Jane was silent, so I continued. "You know that I admire Bruce tremendously. I think he's one of the brightest students in the school. And I certainly hope this little episode won't stop him from fighting for what he believes is right. But, there's a proper way to battle."

Jane was wavering but, knowing her sun sign, I did not expect any capitulation. What would come later would probably be some sort of redirection of the same marvelous Aquarian spark of enthusiasm and humanitarianism.

It has already come. Jane and Bruce are the leaders of a

176

new black student's league in school, fighting for changes in textbooks and curriculum. An Aquarius in an Aquarian age simply cannot lose!

Disciplining and Motivating Aquarius

Aquarius is the sign of the seeker after truth. It is a probing, humane, and sociable sign. The typical Aquarian has an extraordinary scope and a refreshingly open mind. With a warm friendliness and a degree of tranquility, Aquarius searches for the good and the true. He is willing to learn from anyone and eager to pass on what he has learned. His symbol is the water-bearer, pouring out refreshment and quenching the thirst. Like the water he pours, his thoughts and emotions are liquid, ready to be absorbed where they fall.

We are currently living in the astrological age of Aquarius and experiencing the influence of this eleventh sign. We are witnessing a rebirth of humanism and philosophy. Not all of us may agree with some of the manifestations of this age, even though we might be in agreement with the spirit of the age. We may subscribe to the new freedoms but condemn the excesses. Apply this same thinking to your Aquarian child. He is a delightful youngster but there are times when he goes too far. At other times, you may approve of what he is after, but disapprove of the methods he uses. Too often, Aquarius uses the goal to justify the means.

Aquarian youngsters can be unpredictable, so you can anticipate some problems with an offspring born under this sun sign. You never know what they will do next, or what new notion has suddenly influenced their thinking. They may love and defend you today and condemn you tomorrow as tyrannical and repressive. They are given to sudden changes of thought and attitude. There are times when Aquarius must be reminded who is the boss. Don't waste words. When your Aquarian needs discipline, attend to it at once, quickly and decisively.

Aquarian children have an ability to get away with things that would incur parental wrath if other children were involved. When brothers and sisters accuse parents of being partial, it is often to an Aquarian child. Perhaps it is their warmth and good nature that protects them, but parents should guard against their partiality and disturbing favoritism, and distribute justice equally to all their children. And don't think that a clever Aquarius doesn't recognize this advantage.

Rudy, for instance, is not only an Aquarian but he is the youngest child. Both these things have insulated him from potential correction. Even his parents admit that they will tolerate things from him that they would never have allowed with their other children. An Aquarian can become easily spoiled and parents should recognize this fact.

Another accusation brought against this sign is that they tend to fritter away time and talent. They often miss opportunities through procrastination and deliberate neglect. They tend to forget details and concern themselves with the larger concepts. Parents should recognize this when it occurs and prod their Aquarian into action.

On the positive side, the Aquarian is kindly and humane. He is perhaps the most objective sign of the Zodiac and can wrest himself from a totally interior point of view. For this reason, the Aquarian youngster can understand your reasoning and appreciate your opinions. He may not always agree but he will not turn you off. In guiding him and motivating him, a parent can always be assured of a fair hearing and an objective evaluation from the Aquarian child.

An appreciation for the universal and the great concepts of justice, love, beauty, and truth is typical of the Aquarian sun sign. Aquarius has a feeling for humanity and for all its foibles and accomplishments. The Aquarian is world-oriented. As the Aquarian child matures, this social concern will become more pronounced and can be employed to motivate a vocational choice.

Many Aquarians have a habit of saying the wrong thing at the wrong time. They ask tactless questions and offer imprudent opinions. This is never done with malice and is usually well intended. They seem to lack the intuition to allow certain things unspoken. A good deal of their time may be spent in getting out of uncomfortable situations which they have created. Parents will notice this trait at a very early age and should try to teach tact.

Eleven-year-old Sally told her aunt that she was fat. The aunt was appalled and the parents horrified. This is not unusual for Sally. She often says the truth too bluntly. In the beginning, her parents thought it amusing, but now they live in fear of what Sally may say. This is an undesirable habit that should not be allowed to develop. However, if used wisely and in conjunction with the Aquarian social consciousness, much good can be accomplished.

Charles Dickens was an Aquarian and his outspokenness about the social problems of his time helped bring about reform. Again, sun sign characteristics can be used in either a positive or negative way.

PISCES

Every night after dinner, 13-year-old Jonathan would zoom off to the school playground to watch the older boys play basketball on the outdoor courts—his parents thought. What they didn't realize, at first, was that Jonathan was becoming a hanger-on to the older boys. He enjoyed being the butt of their derision more than he enjoyed being one of the boys with his own age group.

Then, one evening Jonathan complained of feeling dizzy when he arrived home. When his parents investigated, it was found that he'd been smoking a cigar which the older boys had insisted he light up, trying to get him sick.

"What other things have the older boys taught you?" his mother asked.

"Nothing!" Jonathan responded, so vehemently that his mother knew there was probably a great deal more. After much probing, it turned out that the boys had also talked him into writing four-letter words on the school wall. And, even more frightening, he'd been maneuvered into puffing on a marijuana reefer once!

Jonathan's mother was frantic. She came to see me to ask how to cope with the situation. She explained that he had a long history of being easily influenced by other people, especially older boys.

I identified Jonathan as a Pisces immediately. In addition to his being susceptible to control, he also knows how to please both his teachers and his parents. His mother claims that he can "wrap me around his little finger" and his teachers always seem pleased with his efforts.

Jonathan is changeable and unsteady. He can be easily talked into something because he's never quite sure of what he should do or what he should believe.

He has artistic ability and a good color sense. The bulletin boards he does for his teacher are tasteful and clever. He has thoughts of being an interior decorator and his mother says that he reads her home decorating magazines with great interest.

Jonathan procrastinates and never does today what can be put off until tomorrow. He frequently hands in school assignments late and loses grade points for it. His teachers say that if he could control his procrastination, his academic record would improve considerably.

Typical of Pisces, Jon likes the water, and swimming is his favorite sport.

The problem obviously was going to be to figure out a way to channel Jonathan's tendency to be swayed by others into constructive behavior without denying this Pisces the pleasure of contact with older people.

I hit on the idea of age-structured groups which would serve the purpose of allowing the boy to make more contact with children of his own age while still allowing for contact with more mature people. The Boy Scouts, the YMCA, participation in class clubs which had teacher advisers in attendance—all of these seemed to prove the answer.

Jonathan's parents and I subtly directed him into these directions. Before very long, he was finding that there just wasn't enough time to make it down to the playground in the evenings.

For all I know, the new Jonathan may still be smoking pot and writing nasty things on the school wall. But, if it's any consolation to his parents, at least he's doing it with his own peer group.

Disciplining and Motivating Pisces

Pisces is a water sign. It is sensitive, kind, and often unlucky. The symbol of Pisces is the fish swimming in either direction. This signifies the ambiguity of Pisces, caught by the currents and carried away by the tides.

Due to the intense sensitivity of Pisces, it is a difficult sign to discipline. Caution must be used in your choice of disciplinary action. Perhaps the most effective way to handle an errant Pisces child is the assignment of extra chores. The more mundane these chores, the better. An extra week of taking out the trash or a spell of sweeping the yard will return Pisces to cooperation and control. Never isolate Pisces in his room since he will probably enjoy being alone for a while. And never scold too harshly. Pisces loves to suffer and play the role of the misunderstood child. Load Pisces up with responsibilities and obligations and you will get more favorable results. Jeff's parents made the mistake of confining him to his room. Unfortunately, they did not understand their Pisces' personality and they discovered that their method simply did not work. The Pisces is indifferent about any restrictions or limitations imposed upon him. He tends to live within himself and he finds himself good company. Actually, Jeff preferred being alone and it was more a pleasure than a punishment.

The Pisces likes to achieve and parents will experience relatively little difficulty in motivating achievement. However, there may be some fringe problems to contend with. One of the most interesting is Pisces' stage fright. Many Pisces youngsters are overcome with an intense and unreasonable apprehension before a critical situation. They may freeze during a test or go to pieces when asked to perform. This is something that they cannot control and which will require sympathy and understanding.

Another Pisces shortcoming is despondency over failure. When your Pisces youngster has failed, it will take on the proportions of a tragedy. He may feel that he can never succeed again and become exceedingly depressed. The only way to help him in a situation like this is to humor him. Do not argue or try to change his thinking. This is an emotional response and must be counteracted with emotional weapons. Joke, laugh, and take his failure lightly. Hopefully, your good humor may become infectious. For instance, after Ellen was rejected for the school hockey team, she retreated into a dark, deep mood. Her mother made the mistake of joining her in her disappointment. Ellen's depression deepened and eventually made her physically ill. Never add coal to a Pisces emotional fire.

There are some astrologers who claim that Shakespeare's Hamlet was a Pisces. Whether this claim be true or false, the Danish prince certainly has Pisces characteristics and could be used as a Pisces prototype. His despondency intensifies throughout the play and eventually destroys him.

Pisces is not the strongest sun sign but it is the most internal and subjective. Pisces retreats within himself and searches inward rather than reaching out. In this age of drug abuse, the parents of a Pisces teenager must be especially on guard. This subjectivity of Pisces makes the sign more prone to experimenting with drugs and desirous of psychedelic experiences. Be certain that your Pisces son or daughter is made clearly aware of the dangers of narcotics. Pisces' introspective yearnings are too often translated into cravings for escape from reality.

On a more favorable note, there are astrologers who say that Pisces is the sun sign of saints and mystics. It is a psychic sign, capable of ceaseless devotion and heroic self-sacrifice. Its introspection can be expressed in meditation and its sensitivity can be expressed in reaching others. The Pisces is capable of great spirituality.

Many parents of Pisces children recognize this spirituality while their children are still quite young. Properly motivated, the Pisces child can develop this spirituality and direct it into some humanitarian or inspirational activity. On the other hand, the same spirituality could drift off into a misdirected interest in the unreal. The way in which the twig is bent is the way in which the tree will grow.

8

Helping Your Child in School

There are two ways to train a horse. One is called bronco busting and the other is called gentling. You bronco bust a horse by forcibly saddling and bridling him. Then a rider mounts him and the contest is on. It's horse against rider, as the animal kicks and bucks, trying to unseat his burden. The rider holds on, tightening the reins to control the animal through pain. After his spirit is somewhat broken and his mouth raw and bleeding, the horse usually relents. The rider represents force and the animal learns to submit to that force.

In gentling, a horse is approached in an opposite way. The trainer leads him step by step toward the acceptance of his task. He tries to establish a trust and friendship between

185

man and the animal. The horse is saddled only after he has become accustomed to lighter weights and is rewarded for good behavior by feeding and petting. Gentle patience is the tone of the entire training procedure. This is the method used on thoroughbreds and by people who value their animals.

The same methods can be applied to working with children. One is impersonal and demanding while the other is gentle and considerate. Obviously, the ideal way is the latter, because it is positive rather than negative. It strives to lead children willingly to goals rather than force them unwillingly to accept goals. It is the best way to teach children. Yet, many parents feel that a child must be broken like a horse. This may work but it can be a bitter and inhuman experience.

Too many parents and teachers stress inadequacies rather than capabilities and focus attention on a child's weaknesses rather than his strengths. He is constantly reminded of what he can't do rather than praised for what he can do. No doubt, most parents would like their children to do well in all school subjects but schools are all too familiar with the parents who ignore the A's and B's only to bewail the C's and F's.

"She didn't even say anything about my good marks!" said one child after his report card was returned to school. And who among us can excel in everything? Children have capabilities and shortcomings and parents must recognize this. In many homes report card days are unhappy experiences for both parent and child. Naturally, parents want children to do well, but children do not always meet this expectation. Every report card cannot represent ultimate effort. Being human, children will fluctuate in their effort and achievement. Again, the grades given to a child are truly representative of his ability and an honest, objective evaluation. To insist that the youngster do better may be asking for frustration and disappointment. It may be saddling the child with

186

a burden he is not ready to carry. It is important for parents to evaluate their children and set realistic goals for them. The sun sign descriptions can help us with this and guide in understanding.

The attitudes of parents are most important in helping a child to learn. If the child thinks you see him as a dummy, he will not disappoint you. On the other hand, if you help him to accept himself and capitalize on his strong points, your child's self-image will improve and so will his school work. What you think of him counts very much.

Recent studies show that children react to the expectations of teachers and parents. They become, in fact, what you want them to become. They seem to sense your evaluation of their ability and they respond accordingly. One child complained to his teacher, "Nothing I do ever pleases her." In this case, it is the mother who has failed, not the child.

We all need encouragement and understanding if we are to succeed and be happy. Always approach your child positively. Negative thinking brings negative results. Young people want to please their parents and have their approval, but they must also be themselves. It is impossible to be yourself when others are making unrealistic demands on you. Parents have it within their power to make school easy or hard for their children, depending on their attitudes and their faith in the child.

Equally important is the attitude toward the school itself. The child knows how his parents see his school and he will adopt their views. "That lousy school!" or "Who does that teacher think she is!" are damaging remarks and dangerous opinions. Too many parents are too free with their criticisms. No matter how poor you may think the school is, your opinion should be kept from the child. A youngster must know that you trust his school if he is to succeed in the classroom. He can only succeed in an atmosphere of confidence, never in a climate of suspicion and condemnation. He needs to know that you support his school and his teachers.

Finally, surround your child with a richness of experience and sensation. Allow him to use his senses to gain information about the world around him. Touching an animal, smelling a flower, tasting a new food, and listening to the sounds of life are all learning experiences. They help to train the senses—the organs of learning. Encourage him to observe everything around him and to use his sight, hearing, smell, and touch as instruments of knowing. Give him experiences that will enrich his understanding of life and of the world in which he lives. Take him on walks, talk to him, read to him, and share with him. All these things will aid him in learning. The richer his experiences and the keener his senses, the better his chances for success in school. A child must be prepared for formal instruction and this is where the parent can play a vital role.

The sun signs of astrology can be of immense service in this regard. A parent can capitalize on the insatiable curiosity of Sagittarius, on the probing mind of Aquarius, the cleverness of Gemini, and the earthiness of Taurus. He can put the enthusiasm of Aries to work and channel the sensitivity of Cancer. He can expect opposition from Leo, cooperation from Capricorn, independence from Scorpio, and alertness from Libra. He will find the Virgo discriminating and may have to push the Pisces.

Your children's sun signs offer you direction in helping your children in this journey through school to adulthood and maturity.

9

Planning Your Child's Sun Sign Future

ARIES

CAREER

As the Arien child grows up, it would be wise to steer him into an active life. Don't suggest he become a bookkeeper. That would be much too dull. Suggest an occupation that will catch his fancy and release his fantastic energy. Notice what the Arien child wants to be when he grows up. He's one who wants to be a fireman, an astronaut, or a deep-sea diver. He thrives on activity, change, and the unknown. He is fascinated by the new and untried. Any occupation that is not fixed or static is for the Arien. He likes change and daily adventure. He enjoys meeting new people and relishes the unexpected. Nothing as fixed as office routine would hold his interest. If your Arien child is to be happy with an occupation, guide him into something that stimulates change and newness. The dramatic arts, fashion, banking, and executive positions should interest him.

EDUCATION

Aries can adjust to any school or college, whether large or small. The big university or the country campus will have equal appeal as long as he likes his course of study. If given the selection, Aries will tend to select the large university or a city college. The small college may not offer the excitement he seeks.

FAMOUS ARIES PERSONALITIES
Arturo Toscanini, Leopold Stokowski, Gloria Swanson, Joan Crawford, Claire Booth Luce, Dean Rusk, Nikita Khrushchev, Thomas Jefferson, Eugene McCarthy, Marlon Brando, Charles Chaplin, Julie Christie, Tennessee Williams, Peter Ustinov, Vincent Van Gogh, Werner Von Braun, and Harold Stassen.

TAURUS

CAREER

Taurus feels happiest where there is security and some outlet for artistic expression. Occupations associated with finance are best suited to this sign, even if it be bookkeeping or accounting, as long as some after-hour hobby provides an aesthetic outlet. Help the Taurus child to develop some hobby or interest that will carry over into adult life. Taurus makes a fine administrator because he can organize well and loves detail. A military career might also attract him because of its firm structure. Many Taurus people establish successful careers in the entertainment industry since they offer security along with artistic expression.

EDUCATION

Taurus children are naturals for military school or any highly regimented institution. They work well in a firm framework of operation. They are not the students who would respond to a permissive atmosphere. Summerhill was not meant for Taurus!

> FAMOUS TAURUS PERSONALITIES
> *Bing Crosby, James Stewart, Henry Fonda, James Mason, William Shakespeare, Salvador Dali, Johannes Brahms, Ulysses S. Grant, Orson Welles, Margot Fonteyn, Sigmund Freud, Willy Mays, Vladimir Nabokov, Barbra Streisand, Robespierre, Hitler, and Shirley Temple.*

CANCER

CAREER

Cancers are fine merchandisers who are able to take any product and sell it. They are also capable restaurateurs and hotel managers. Anything having to do with the home or hospitality will appeal to Cancer. They make excellent decorators, stewardesses, real estate salesmen, or furniture dealers. Cancer also meets success in the secondhand market, especially in antiques. Many top antiques experts have been born under the Cancerian sign. Cancers make excellent teachers because they have an instinctive understanding of children.

When it is time to go away to school, never send Cancer to a large university. This sign needs intimacy and the comforts of home. He will succeed best in a small college or school. In a large school, his chances for success are narrowed unless he can establish himself in a group or form a close tie with some teacher.

FAMOUS CANCER PERSONALITIES
Ginger Rogers, Lena Horne, Red Skelton, Milton Berle, Helen Keller, Anne Morrow Lindbergh, Ernest Hemingway, Marcel Proust, Yul Brynner, Ingmar Bergman, the Duke of Windsor, John D. and Nelson Rockefeller, Gina Lollobrigida, Phyllis Diller, Julius Caesar, and Ringo Starr.

GEMINI

CAREER

Gemini is the sign of the super-salesmen. They are fast talkers and have keen minds capable of quick decisions and fast judgments. Any profession or occupation requiring this ability will be perfect for the Gemini. Gemini has produced many doctors, lawyers, and executives as a result of this capacity for effective handling of emergency situations. Another fine career for the Gemini is any phase of the publishing or mass media industry. Gemini blossoms in an open, free environment.

EDUCATION

He is best suited to the more progressive kind of school or to some form of work-study program. The Gemini will not be happy in any tightly organized situation where excessive demands are made of him. He wants freedom of movement and freedom of decision. A large university offering a diversity of courses or a small, progressive college will be best for Gemini's higher education. Steer him away from conservative, highly-structured institutions.

FAMOUS GEMINI PERSONALITIES
John Fitzgerald Kennedy, Queen Victoria, Frank Lloyd Wright, Bob Hope, Marilyn Monroe, the Duchess of Windsor, the Duke of Edinburgh, Bob Dylan, Judy Garland, Françoise Sagan, Walt Whitman, Paul Gauguin, Bennett Cerf, John Dillinger, and Paul McCartney.

LEO

CAREER

Leo the extrovert is happiest in any occupation that offers an opportunity for him to demonstrate his abilities. Public service is a natural for Leo and he will thrive on this kind of work, no matter how difficult or demanding it may be. Leo likes to be the boss so he should aim for an administrative position or a vocation that allows supervision. Leo also enjoys recognition and acclaim. Many politicians are Leos and many leading sports figures have been born under the sign. Leo likes the limelight and the adoration of the crowd. His happiest hours will be spent in the high atmosphere of policy formation, manipulating public opinion, or pleasing the crowd.

EDUCATION

The college best suited to a Leo is one that will allow him to roar. As long as there are lots of extracurricular activities,

Leo will be happy. He wants to show off his prowess and must be given the opportunity.

VIRGO

CAREER

Being perfectionists, Virgos love detailed work. They derive great satisfaction from output that can be measured and seen. Virgo girls make excellent nurses, secretaries, and business executives. The boys enjoy the skilled trades and can become excellent craftsmen. As Virgo likes to be of service to his fellow men, a career in any branch of the medical profession or social sciences will bring great rewards. Virgo also makes a fine technologist and engineer.

EDUCATION

Virgo is a born student and enjoys an academic environment. He would probably do best in a university or in a fine technical school. He respects proficiency and ability and demands much from his teachers. A poor or "second-best" school will engender his contempt. Whatever Virgo decides to be, he will want the best training available. It would be well to see that he gets it because he will put this training to good use.

Taft, Lyndon B. Johnson, Leonard Bernstein, Peter Sellers, Sophia Loren, Grandma Moses, Greta Garbo, F. Scott Fitzgerald, William Saroyan, Lauren Bacall, Ingrid Bergman, Arthur Godfrey, D. H. Lawrence, Walter Reuther, Goethe, Tolstoy, Lafayette, and Van Johnson.

LIBRA

CAREER

There must be some expression of the beautiful in anything that Libra does or he will be unhappy. The Libran also values peace and harmony and will work hard to obtain it. For this reason, social work and religious vocations appeal to this sign. This desire for beauty can find an outlet in working with flowers, interior decorating, designing, and architecture. Any work activity that brings about a closer cooperation among people or produces some expression of beauty and order will appeal to Libra. It has been claimed by astrologers that many of the famous peacemakers and labor arbitrators were born under this sign.

EDUCATION

Libra needs a small, quiet school, perhaps out in the country, or one operated by a religious order. He needs a place and time to meditate and the rush and confusion of an urban school might undo him.

FAMOUS LIBRA PERSONALITIES
Helen Hayes, Isadora Duncan, Julie Andrews, Brigitte Bardot, Ed Sullivan, Sara Bernhardt, Truman Capote, Oscar Wilde, Thomas Wolfe, David Ben-Gurion, Marcello Mastroianni, Eleanor Roosevelt,

Mickey Mantle, T. S. Eliot, Franz Liszt, Dwight D. Eisenhower, Nietzsche, Gandhi, and John Lennon.

SCORPIO

CAREER

The Scorpio is a born investigator and is brimming with bodily energy. He will enjoy any occupation that involves ferreting out flaws or searching out hidden motives. The world of high finance fascinates him as does law and law enforcement. Many Scorpios find an outlet for their abilities in the military life or in some kind of close mechanical work. Because of Scorpio's love of activity and physical motion, he makes an excellent sportsman or physical educator. He might also find satisfaction in physical therapy.

EDUCATION

The Scorpio student is happiest when he can pursue his own interests. He will not respond to a school where the curriculum is fixed or where there is little academic flexibility. When he can choose his own subject matter, or at least a greater part of it, Scorpio's chances for academic success are ensured.

FAMOUS SCORPIO PERSONALITIES
Robert F. Kennedy, Martin Luther, Teddy Roosevelt, Charles DeGaulle, Grace Kelly, Richard Burton, Katherine Hepburn, Ethel Waters, Mike Nichols, Johnny Carson, Billy Graham, Jonas Salk, Chiang Kaishek, Prince Charles, Indira Gandhi, Marie Antoinette, Nehru, Picasso, and Hedy Lamar.

SAGITTARIUS

CAREER

The Sagittarian likes to work alone and operate independently. He would make a fine independent businessman who could be his own boss. This sign also enjoys talking, so any occupation utilizing vocal ability is a natural choice for Sagittarius. He will find satisfaction in teaching or in the communications industry. Sagittarius also loves to travel and any job taking him to different regions or other lands will be certain to bring contentment. Few Sagittarians are happy too close to home. After your Sagittarian finishes school, he will probably move away from home. Realize that this is his nature and not a rejection of you. It would be wise to encourage your Sagittarian to study a foreign language so that the probability of his being employed in another country will be increased. This he will enjoy and he will thank you for it.

EDUCATION

Send Sagittarius away to school and the further the better. Never suggest that he attend the local college or the state university. He needs and wants distance and his chances for success will be increased.

FAMOUS SAGITTARIUS PERSONALITIES
Flaubert, Spinoza, Mark Twain, Pope John XXIII, James Thurber, Frank Sinatra, Mary Martin, Walt Disney, Ludwig van Beethoven, Maria Callas, Betty Grable, Noel Coward, Sammy Davis, Joe DiMaggio, J. Paul Getty, Andrew Carnegie, Disraeli, Winston

Churchill, Adam Clayton Powell, John V. Lindsay, William Buckley, Jr., and David Susskind.

CAPRICORN

CAREER

Capricorn is an organizer and likes any situation in which he can employ his ability to sort, classify, and list. As he values a good reputation, any position of trust is perfectly suited to him. A job or profession that can combine organizational ability with a need for trust and confidence would be perfect. Capricorn makes an honest and upright public servant and would be an asset to any corporation or organization requiring a trustworthy employee.

EDUCATION

Capricorn will do best in a small school or college where he is not lost in the crowd. As he likes to please his teachers, he needs their recognition. A small school would offer him this identity. Capricorn is a small-town boy at heart and may be put off by a large university or institution.

FAMOUS CAPRICORN PERSONALITIES
Martin Luther King, Benjamin Franklin, Alexander Hamilton, Woodrow Wilson, Richard M. Nixon, Dr. Albert Schweitzer, Pablo Casals, Howard Hughes, Steve Allen, Cary Grant, Humphrey Bogart, Marlene Dietrich, Henry Miller, Rudyard Kipling, Sir Isaac Newton, Barry Goldwater, Mao Tse-tung, Joan of Arc, and J. Edgar Hoover.

AQUARIUS

Aside from being the sign of the inventor, the Aquarian likes to be with people. His social instinct is strong, so any occupation that allows him to be with others is bound to please. Social work, teaching, selling, public relations, and organizational work are suited to the Aquarian nature. The Aquarian is also attracted to the fashion industry and many Aquarians are designers, jewelers, and furriers. They are also found in the magazine business as this permits them to convey ideas to a large audience. The Aquarian expresses himself through other people.

EDUCATION

Aquarius will enjoy the excitement of a large school and the sophistication of a metropolitan campus. The larger the institution, the better, and the more students, the better. Aquarius finds great comfort in being with large numbers of people and in the excitement of mass education. He is more at home in the large lecture hall than in the intimate classroom.

FAMOUS AQUARIUS PERSONALITIES
Franklin D. Roosevelt, Adlai Stevenson, Abraham Lincoln, Charles Lindbergh, Charles Darwin, Somerset Maugham, Norman Mailer, Lewis Carroll, James Joyce, Mozart, Segovia, Galileo, Thomas Edison, General Omar Bradley, Vanessa Redgrave, Tallulah Bankhead, Jeanne Moreau, Clark Gable, Leontyne

Price, John Barrymore, Mia Farrow, Ann Sothern, and Ronald Reagan.

PISCES

CAREER

Being the in-tune sign, Pisces can enter most professions and accept most occupations. Vocationally, Pisces has the ability to fit in well under any circumstances and it is difficult to suggest a certain vocational talent. Many artists are born under this sign and many Pisces children may enter artistic fields.

EDUCATION

As to school, Pisces best enjoys a small, intimate institution. A Pisces can certainly adjust to a large campus but will feel more comfortable with smallness and intimacy. If attending a larger institution is unavoidable, the Pisces can accept such a negative situation and live with it better than any other sign.

FAMOUS PISCES PERSONALITIES
Senator Edward Kennedy, George Washington, Grover Cleveland, Edna St. Vincent Millay, Robert Lowell, Earl Warren, Svetlana Stalin, Albert Einstein, Anthony Armstrong-Jones, Mickey Spillane, Edward Albee, Michelangelo, Renoir, Caruso, Nijinsky, John Steinbeck, Rex Harrison, Harry Belafonte, Rudolph Nureyev, Dinah Shore, Elizabeth Taylor, Handel, Chopin, and George Harrison.

10

Your Sun Sign vs. Your Children's

I know a Virgo father who is aware of his sun sign tendency to become absorbed in his business, often to the exclusion of his family. He has two sons, one a 7-year-old Pisces and the other a 12-year-old Cancer. Both these signs need lots of parental affection and, being boys, they especially need the companionship of their father. Knowing this and knowing himself, this father has made a point of spending every weekend with his family. Despite the frequent temptation to spend a Saturday at the office, this wise man keeps his weekend appointment faithfully. His knowledge of himself and his family has paid dividends in two happy sons.

A neighbor of mine was born under the sun sign Taurus. This sign enjoys good food and likes to eat. If she followed her natural bent, her dinner table would be laden with rich foods and both she and her family would be overweight. She is very careful of the family diet, especially for the sake of her two teenage daughters. They are both attractive and slim. She once confessed that she couldn't wait for her children to grow up and leave home so that she could cook to her heart's delight. Yet she was determined not to teach them bad eating habits merely to satisfy her own inclination. Whether you call it good nutrition or good astrology, it is certainly an example of good understanding.

The compatibility of the various sun signs is open to wide interpretation and is an area of much disagreement among professional astrologers. As I have previously explained, in an attempt to establish some basis for grouping the twelve signs of the Zodiac, the ancient astrologers distributed the signs among four basic elements that were thought to make up the universe—Fire, Earth, Air, and Water. Convinced that everything was composed of some combination of these elements, they decided to match the characteristics of the signs to the characteristics of the four elements. They reasoned from their observations of nature, that each sign must have a more predominant element in its composition and that this element ruled the sign.

For example, the impulsive, energetic Aries, like a dancing flame, was seen as a Fire sign. The restlessness of Gemini, much like the inconstant wind, was an Air sign. Easily influenced Pisces, like liquid assuming the shape of its container, was labeled a Water sign and earthy Taurus was obviously an Earth sign. Each sun sign personality was assigned to its corresponding element and the twelve signs were divided equally among the four elements.

Here, again, are those groups:
Fire signs—Aries, Leo, Sagittarius

Earth signs—Taurus, Virgo, Capricorn
Air signs—Gemini, Libra, Aquarius
Water signs—Cancer, Scorpio, Pisces

Some astrologers say that the signs are in tune with the others in their group and thus are best for each other. As they share common characteristics and have similar temperaments, they are thought to be in harmony. This may be true, but sometimes like personalities can rub each other the wrong way, causing competition and conflict.

A friend of mine is a Leo and her teenage daughter is an Aries. These are two Fire signs, each aggressive and each demanding her own way in things. The household is the scene of frequent turmoil as two similar personalities express themselves. And to make matters worse, the poor father is a Pisces and is victimized by both. I have warned my friend repeatedly that the day may come when the two Fire signs may make the Water sign boil!

On the other hand, a Cancer father in my immediate family gets along beautifully with his Pisces son. They seem to possess an instinctive understanding of each other and have formed an ideal relationship.

Some astrologers claim that the Fire signs and the Air signs do not harmonize as well among their own, as do the Earth and Water signs. They probably figure that two fires can only make things hotter and that two airs can only stir things up more.

There are a host of interpretations based on the properties of the elements. There are those who say that a Water sign will diminish a Fire sign while it makes an Earth sign more fertile and productive. We all know that Fire and Water do not mix but, using the same logic, Earth and Water made mud! However, if this thinking is accepted, then Cancer, Pisces, and Scorpio are good for Taurus, Virgo, and Capricorn, but spell trouble for Aries, Leo, and Sagittarius. Continuing the same thinking, an Air sign will make a Fire sign burn more brightly but may dry and parch an Earth sign. Here, Gemini, Libra, and Aquarius are complementary to Aries, Leo and Sagittarius, but may harm Taurus, Virgo, and Capricorn.

Still another group of astrologers insists that the opposing signs are those directly across from each other on the wheel of the Zodiac. These six combinations would be Aries-Libra, Taurus-Scorpio, Gemini-Sagittarius, Cancer-Capricorn, Leo-Aquarius, and Virgo-Pisces. If what they claim is true, these would make for a poor child-babysitter combination.

I know one case where this happened, when a simple situation in the hands of opposing signs grew out of proportion. Eleven-year-old Cancer liked to eat burned toast in the morning. For some strange reason he wanted his bread reduced to charcoal. His mother had always indulged his whim but he met strong opposition one weekend. Left in the charge of a Capricorn babysitter, he was denied his black toast. Proper Capricorn insisted on properly toasted bread. The spoiled Cancer pushed each piece of toast back down into the toaster and filled the kitchen with billows of smoke. The Capricorn babysitter interpreted this as a defiance of her authority. Meanwhile, Cancer, viewing the circumstances as cruel persecution, began to cry. This was the start of a disastrous weekend and the abrupt end of a dollar-an-hour Cancer-Capricorn combination.

By the same token, however, we know that opposites sometimes attract. Like the positive and negative poles of a magnet, they can have an affinity for each other. Perhaps the qualities that one might lack are found in the other and the combination may produce a highly complementary pattern.

A Taurus-Scorpio relationship is said by some to be a most auspicious union, as the qualities of both signs working together bring success and security. I know two teenagers who were born under these signs and seem to exemplify this premise. They have been "going steady" since ninth grade and their relationship seems to have a depth and maturity beyond their years. They are exceedingly loyal to one another and deeply considerate.

There are many other instances of relationships, friendships, and partnerships where one sun sign serves the other. Perhaps it is more a case of knowledge and compassion being used to good advantage. After all, the more we know ourselves and those about us, the greater our chances for happiness. Often, opposite traits under the guidance and control of reason can work together with surprisingly good results.

As Mother Goose put it:

> Jack Sprat could eat no fat,
> His wife could eat no lean;
> And so betwixt them both,
> They licked the platter clean.

The sun signs can serve as another useful tool in understanding and working with the complexities of the human personality. When used as an extra dimension, the sun signs become meaningful. When used as a fatalistic measure, they become harshly restrictive. Let's assume that the Virgo-Pisces relationship is a poor combination, as some astrologers would have us believe. Few among us would accept this as a reason for a Virgo mother to neglect her Pisces child or give up trying to help him. Astrology should never be an excuse for irresponsibility. We are what we are and we must go on from there.

There is no room for any lack of compassion and hope in anyone working with children. Yet, common experience dictates that not all personalities are accommodating and that people do disagree. The fact is that people are different, but we must find opportunities in these differences. We must extend ourselves and learn to appreciate the rhythm of our children's ways. Understanding them is the first step in learning to live with them.

A mother once told me, "I love my child but I don't always like him!" This is often true, for love is really nothing more than a high degree of tolerance. We may not always like our problem child but we still go on loving him and trying to understand him. It follows that a parent who understands a child will be better able to accept his shortcomings and limitations. But more than this, a parent who understands herself as well will be bound to make more accurate estimates of the interaction between parent and child. It is here that the sun signs offer help.

A Cancer mother who knows the urging of her sign to hold on to her children will be better able to let go. The mother who understands the nature of her Sagittarius will be better able to cope with his restlessness. In parenthood, as in most spheres of human endeavor, knowledge is power.

The sun sign personality profiles help us to know ourselves and to know our children—the only sure formula for successful parenthood.

11

Your Child in the Aquarian Age

Astrologers tell us that the world has entered the Aquarian Age. The movement of the vernal equinox in a westward direction is bringing the world from 2000 years in the Zodiac sign of Pisces to the next 2000 years in Aquarius. Pisces was the age of skepticism and doubt; Aquarius is the age of inspiration and accomplishment.

According to astrological sources, the world entered the Aquarian Age about 1905 and, with it, we entered an age of scientific accomplishment and artistic progress. The Aquarian sign is concerned with the betterment of mankind and the improvement of society. It is a humanitarian sign and one involved in human progress. The world is just beginning to feel the impact of the dawning of this age, and already Aquarian progress has taken place.

Space exploration, the war against poverty, student rebellion, the reform of religion—these are all manifestations of the influence of Aquarius. Aquarius is honesty, reform, change, and improvement. And it has just begun! The best is yet to come! The world will not be truly under the full influence of Aquarius until the year 2000 and that time will see the real impact of the Aquarian Age.

If the influence of this strong social sign has been felt up to now, think what changes and reforms it will cause in the future. The future of the world is full of excitement and promise. The Aquarian Age will bring about a new world filled with new ideas and novel approaches. The old problems that have plagued mankind since the beginning of time will find fresh and new solutions in this great age and mankind will reach its highest peak. For the first time in the history of the world, man will be in such complete control of his environment.

The Aquarian Age is the dawning of a new day in the history of the world and has been eagerly awaited by astrologers for centuries. All the ancient astrologers knew of its coming and all predicted great things for our world when the age finally appeared. It was to be a day when peace and love would guide humanity in its decisions and in its course.

What better astrological time in which to live than in the Age of Aquarius? The children of today should be especially thankful. They have been born into the best of astrological climates—a world ruled by Aquarius.

For over two thousand years, mankind has tried in vain to live and practice the ethical ideals of Christianity and the other great religions. He has attempted to love his neighbor and to ensure justice for the least of his brothers. Now, in the Age of Aquarius, this hope can become a reality as men everywhere are guided by this beneficial influence toward a realization of their ancient dreams.

The Aquarian influence will be felt in every activity of men around the globe. Some astrologers even predict the end of war and conflict and the final dawning of an age of peaceful coexistence. This, the dream of centuries, will become a workable rule in the golden age of mankind.

What better time to grow up? What better environment in which to live? Your children will have the rare opportunity to use their talents for the betterment of humanity and direct their energies toward the construction of a new society. Science will develop at an astounding rate and cures will be found for the diseases that have plagued the world. The arts, too, will bring forth a new and exhilarating dimension never before imagined. Psychology will uncover the secrets of the human heart and religion will enter a renewed period of intensity and devotion. Every aspect of human endeavor will benefit from the beneficent influence of Aquarius.

Your child will know a world entirely different from yours. You have only been given a glimpse of the fruit of this fertile vine; its full blossoming and harvest are yet to come. Your child will live in a world of tranquility and understanding and he will be spared the trials and sorrows of his ancestors. Imagine a world with no wars, no hunger and poverty, reduced disease and suffering.

This is the promise of the Aquarian Age and what a promise it is! This is the astrological heritage of your children.

12

The Ten Astrological Commandments of Parenthood

1. *Always Be Consistent*

Use the sun signs to help you set limits. Then, it makes no difference if you are strict or lenient, as long as you remain consistent. Don't be weak one minute and demanding the next. If you have studied your own sun signs as well as your child's, you should be able to establish a workable pattern. Let the child know what you will accept and what you will not accept. When you make a decision, be ready to stick with it.

2. Set a Good Example

Your awareness of your own sun sign will help you to understand yourself and thus impart your true values to your children. You'll teach them best by living up to your teaching. Children are not fooled by lip service. If you want honesty, then you must be honest yourself. If you want consideration for others, then you must be considerate yourself.

3. Respect Your Child

Your child is a human and deserves respect. Anything that lessens his dignity as a human being is an injustice. Humiliation, sarcasm, neglect, and cruelty are sins against any child. A knowledge of the personality traits which may develop in your child through a knowledge of his sun sign may help you to afford him the inherent respect his humanity demands.

4. Be Realistic About Talents and Abilities

Know your child better by studying his sun sign. Don't expect what he cannot deliver. Praise him for things well done, and be realistic about your expectations. Don't try to change his nature. A Pisces can never be a Taurus, no matter how hard you try.

5. Cooperate with the School

Your child's teacher may not know your child's sun sign, but the chances are that the teacher knows children and you should respect that professional knowledge. After all, both you and the school want the best for your child. You both want him to succeed. Try to approach any problem at school with the attitude that teachers are fair and reasonable people, and thus avoid pitting your child against his teacher with misguided belligerence.

6. *Help Your Child Establish Good Habits*

There is an old saying that the way a twig is bent, so the tree will grow. Children need to establish routines of good living. Certain good health habits and social procedures are valuable to every child, regardless of sun sign. Make sure that your child knows them, but make sure that you really know them yourself first.

7. *Don't Get Hysterical Over Misbehavior*

Even the law-abiding Capricorn will misbehave occasionally. Don't fall apart in a crisis. Be calm and remember the advice of your child's sun sign—and your own. Any overreaction will only make things worse.

8. *Uphold Certain Standards*

Remember that sun signs are merely personality descriptions—they should never be used as definitive guides to personal morality. You must establish moral standards for your child to follow, and they've got to be based on more than some vague sun-sign destiny mystique. Let your child know that there are certain things you believe in and hope for him to accept. It's surprising how cooperative children can be when they know you want and need their cooperation.

9. *Know Your Child*

Know his sun sign and know it well. Constantly evaluate your child and never be blind to what is happening under your own nose. Know your own sun sign as well and try to understand how the signs intermesh. But keep trying. Too often a generation gap is a man-made chasm which could have been breached by just a little more positive effort.

10. *Help Your Child Achieve Independence*

Every child is reaching out for independence. The older he grows, the more he wants and needs. Allow him to find his independence by helping him to understand his sun sign. He'll be grateful to you as he flourishes in the positive aspects of his sun sign.